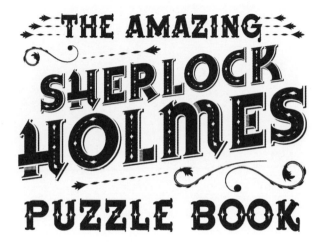

THE AMAZING SHERLOCK HOLMES PUZZLE BOOK

THE AMAZING SHERLOCK HOLMES

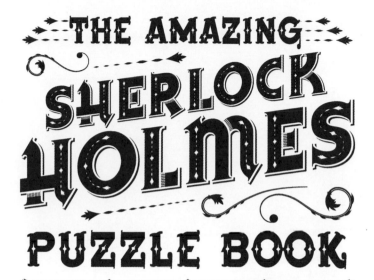

PUZZLE BOOK

A cornucopia of
conundrums inspired
by the world's
greatest detective

Dr Gareth Moore

SIRIUS

SIRIUS

This edition published in 2022 by Arcturus Publishing Limited
26/27 Bickels Yard, 151–153 Bermondsey Street,
London SE1 3HA

ISBN: 978-1-3988-2137-8
AD007165UK

Printed in China

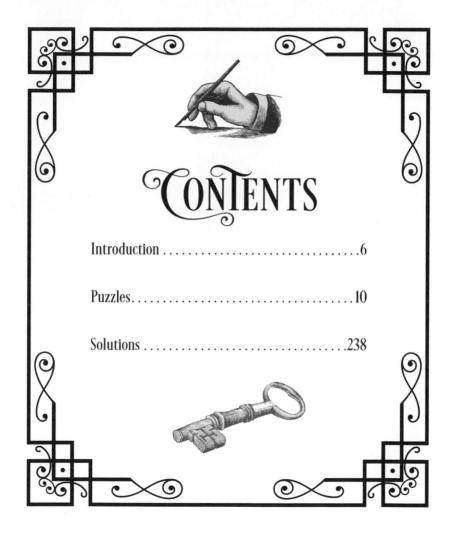

CONTENTS

INTRODUCTION

Dear Reader,

I am delighted to welcome you back to this second volume of our puzzle adventures. I hope that you will find it as intriguing and edifying as my first such compilation, and indeed it is the success of that precursor volume which has led me to put pen to paper once again. It would further have been churlish of me to keep knowledge of our many experiences to myself, for society at large has much to learn from the methods and observations of that most singular gentleman, Mr Sherlock Holmes.

In this book, I relay to you 138 situations in which Holmes and I have found ourselves during the pursuit of our manifold cases. I have presented them in such a way that you can challenge yourself to answer the very same conundrums that caused momentary pause to either myself or Holmes, and I hope that some small enjoyment will be found in your attempts to keep up with the great detective's mind.

Should you not, however, have read our first volume, or have somehow failed to have heard of the detective tour de force that is Mr Sherlock Holmes, let me take a moment to introduce you to him, peccadillos and all.

His signature feature is his towering intellect. His cranial cogitations are majestic in their profundity, often reducing mere mortals, such as you and I, to simple observers. I frequently find myself unable to offer any additional insight into his investigatory activities. Having already solved a mystery, however, he enjoys playing with others in the way that a cat will tease its prey, ensuring that you are never in any doubt as to how superior his own intelligence is to yours. He will also frequently challenge you to reach some conclusion or the other, but it is invariably one that he has long ago passed at the wayside in his own insatiable quest for knowledge.

The challenges in this book are of several different types. Some rely on principles of the mathematical kind, while many need one or more logical deductions to be made from the presented writings. A few make reference to contemporary technology or other new inventions of our Victorian era, and others require abstract thinking to explain some apparently impossible situation. Let me assure you, however, that none require any special knowledge or experience, beyond the wit that the mighty Lord himself gave you as you passed the boundary into this mortal world.

Holmes is rather fond of riddles, so I should also take this opportunity to give you fair warning that at least a few of the challenges require cleverness of the language variety, with a few plays on words and the like. If a puzzle seems unsolvable, it is always worth considering that some cleverness is at play and all is not as it seems. I have also occasionally seen fit to put a small hint into some of the puzzle titles, so if you should ever find yourself stuck then it is always worth considering the true meaning of the title. Perhaps it might be of some small assistance in your hunt for even the most elusive of answers.

Should any of the herein conundrums happen to challenge and perplex you beyond your ken, I have (once again much against Holmes's recommendation, I might add) included full solutions at the back of this volume. Here I have stated the answer as it was originally given to me, and explained any solving mechanism where it was appropriate to do so. This section might, I suggest, be given to a friend or detective colleague to read, so that they can concoct a hint that is slightly less fiendish than those already given you on the puzzle pages.

Each challenge may be tackled on its own, and you may dip in and out of the book at your leisure. The material tells no grand overall story, beyond further documenting the genius of the man I am lucky to call my friend: Mr Sherlock Holmes.

Dr John Watson,
221B Baker Street, London, 1899

The Warrior Women

One day I enjoyed a lunchtime stroll around the streets close to 221B Baker Street. As I meandered through the familiar environs, I began to wonder if I could best Holmes by inventing a riddle of my own. It may have been foolish, but I felt the need to try.

After working on it for a full hour, I returned and presented him with the following challenge:

"Thirty men and two women, dressed in uniforms of black or white, are locked in combat for many hours. The women may be few, but they hold the most power of all those on the battlefield. Who are these warriors?"

Holmes didn't even grant me the satisfaction of a dramatic pause before immediately giving me the answer I had intended.

What did he say?

AN ORDERED SEQUENCE

One day Holmes looked up from a volume he was reading, and I knew that look meant only one thing. He had decided to prove his immense intellect by demonstrating the relative inadequacies of mine. Sighing, I prepared to get it over and done with.

"Watson, tell me this. I observe some initial letters from a sequence I see in this book. All you must do is tell me this: which letter should come next?

"The sequence is thus:

F S T F F S S.

"So tell me. What is next?"

A Hat-Trick

Although it is a rare occurrence, I do find on occasion that Holmes' astounding ability to think logically about this material world can cloud his usually flawless judgement.

We were out hunting one day. This was an activity in which we very rarely engaged, but Holmes had agreed to take part for the chance to try out a new weapon, and I challenged him to a small bet.

I bet Holmes that I would be able to hang my hat and then, having walked 500 yards, turn and shoot a hole straight through the top of it, all while keeping my eyes closed.

Despite knowing me to be an excellent shot, he deemed it near impossible and readily accepted my bet. And yet I won. Easily.

How?

THE STRAND PYRAMID ONE

Holmes was rather an avid reader of *The Strand Magazine*, and I must admit that I would pick my way through it after he had thoroughly informed himself of its contents.

The magazine would, from time to time, include a range of puzzle entertainments, suitable for gentlemen such as ourselves. One that both Holmes and I enjoyed was known as the Strand Pyramid. It was built from words, and the only confusion was that the words themselves were not given, but rather clues. It was up to the reader to discover the words.

To assist in this task, a particular property was noted. Each clue was solved using the same set of letters as the word before, but with the addition of one further letter. The letters could, however, then be jumbled as you pleased. It might also be worth stating that the first clue was always solved by a three-letter word, and that the pyramid was built (somewhat improbably) from the top downward.

Here is the first pyramid puzzle we tackled:

1. Observe
2. Relax
3. Roof overhangs
4. Autumnal fall
5. Quite a few
6. Meat choppers

Can you solve it?

SOCIETY RIDDLES

Given the success my writings have enjoyed, Holmes and I now find ourselves in the public eye. One of the downsides is that we are expected to attend many grand occasions. You might expect this to be a treat, but the truth is that they distract from the important work that we must do.

On the occasions when we do attend, we often must put up with all and sundry coming up to us and inflicting their own criminal theories about what they think *really* happened in such and such a case, or how obvious they think the solution to a particular case was.

And that is not the half of it! I have lost count of the number of times a well-dressed partygoer has attempted to catch us out with a riddle. Usually it is one we have heard before, despite their poor attempt to claim it as their own. One of the most common is this:

"You find me in the past, and I can be created in the present, but the future is never mine. What am I?"

THE GAP YEAR

There is much trouble involving the youths of London, although I do fear that it is not just London but the entire country which is so afflicted. In any case, an altercation in the West End of this city some three winters ago resulted in the death of a young man. Holmes and I happened to be nearby, and being recognized by a passing constable we were asked for our assistance in the matter.

The suspect was a boy who, we guessed, was in his early teens, but he seemed not to know the word for his current age. Instead, he insisted on describing it in a roundabout way.

On the day we question him, he claimed that he was thirteen years old the day before yesterday, and then informed us that next year he would be sixteen.

I thought this seemed impossible when I first heard it, but the boy's answer made sense despite his indirect method of providing it. How is this so?

A STRANGE CASE

One day we were presented with a locked suitcase, with a combination the owner professed to have forgotten. When asked why he did not simply force it open, he claimed that it contained items of such huge sentimental value to him that he could not risk them being damaged. Could we not help him by cracking the combination?

Luckily the lock was of a certain design that Holmes was familiar with, which meant that he could rapidly narrow down the possibilities.

He soon discovered that:

The number had 4 digits which all increased in value from left to right (such as 1258)

No two successive digits had an even difference (such as 2 or 4)

The sum of the digits was 22

There was no 0 in the combination

This narrowed it down to a few options, of which it turned out to be the numerically lowest. What was the combination?

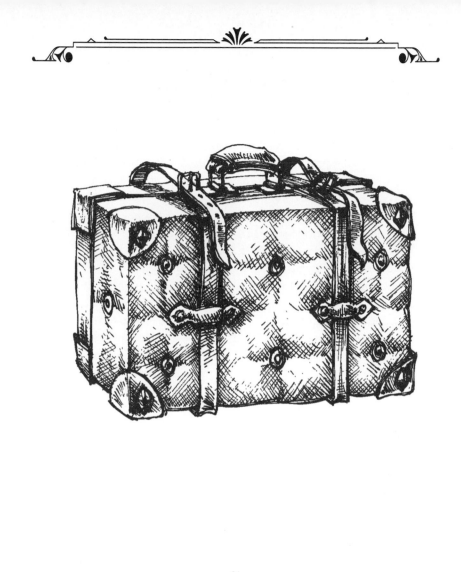

A FAIR AFFAIR

"Have you ever been to a country fair, Watson?" Holmes asked me one day, during a cab ride near the outskirts of London. At that moment it happened that we were passing a row of carts on their way to such a fair.

"A few," I replied, "although they were more of the urban type than the rural."

Holmes seemed in an unusually relaxed mood, for he responded by saying, "Ah yes, but they lack some of the more space-hungry amusements, such as the hot-air balloons or the circus tent. And besides, the city surrounds are so stultifying."

I could hardly imagine Holmes meandering happily among such vagaries as the carousel d'animaux, the hammer bell, and the candied sugar treats, and was about to say so when he interrupted with a jarring change of tone.

"The last fair I attended I saw a dead man. Smack-bang in the middle of a field. He was not part of the fair, but had appeared there overnight.

"He was carrying an unopened package on his back. I have seen death many times, but I must confess that this left its mark. It struck me that even when he was still far from that field, he must have felt a cold chill as he became certain that death was approaching."

Why had the man been so sure he was about to die?

LOOKING APART

Holmes had recently crossed the North Atlantic on the RMS Majestic and now began recounting an encounter with a rival of his, Inspector William Murphy. This gentleman was from Manhattan, and rather too sure of himself for my friend's liking.

Holmes was explaining a particular situation that had exasperated him, saying, "We found ourselves facing opposite directions: him, due West, and I, due East. But as I stood there, I saw in his eyes that—"

"Wait. What do you mean, saw in his eyes?" I managed to interject. "Was there some sort of mirage or reflection that meant you could see each other, even while facing opposite directions?" I asked, somewhat sarcastically. I was sure I had caught Holmes out.

"No, of course not," he responded.

"Well, then, did you turn your heads to see each other?", I persisted.

"No, no. Watson, why are you so stuck on this matter? There was no trickery involved."

Can you explain the situation?

THE HOSPITAL BALL

Holmes and I were visiting a witness on what we had been told might be her deathbed, in an attempt to coax out one last clue to a particularly annoying case that we had been having trouble resolving.

The woman in question had been infuriatingly cryptic with us, presumably in an attempt to protect a loved one. We were asking her about the death of a man she had lived opposite for many years, as we thought it was of significance to the matter.

The woman, however, was more concerned with her own impending death, and had little of any aid to tell us. Even so, we were momentarily thrown when the woman stopped and asked us, "What did I catch and yet can never throw? Nor could any soul."

THE SEWER RIDDLE

I am very sure that I do not earn enough to be subject to the sort of conditions that some investigations require. However, if Holmes believes it to be pertinent to the case, I feel I have no option but to follow him wherever it may be, including into the fetid sewage tunnels that crawl like snakes beneath this city.

During one such visit to the sewer, I tripped on an unseen obstacle and found much of my person covered in the most foul-smelling material, to the point where I needed to be hoisted out of the disgusting pool by Holmes himself. When I emerged, soaked but otherwise unscathed, I was greeted by Holmes in an uncharacteristic fit of laughter.

"Ah, Watson. What a shame. But still, a riddle may help, perhaps?"

I felt that it certainly wouldn't, but he continued nonetheless:

"Certainly this one seems pertinent. Here, Watson: What is it that always tastes better than it smells?"

I tried and then failed to think of some suitable foods, but what was Holmes thinking of?

AN EMOTIVE MOTIVE

Lestrade requested that Holmes and I attend the station for a most shocking case. He wished us to interview a girl who had been arrested for murdering her sister.

Lestrade read us his notes:

"The young woman attended her mother's funeral. (Sad, so sad). Claims that she met a man she had never laid eyes on afore. Family friend. Friend of a friend, perhaps. Claims that she fell madly in love with him. And that's it. That's all she will say. She was unable to find him after the funeral, and tried for years. She is obsessed."

Holmes tutted, and Lestrade paused.

"Allow me to speculate on the matter," said Holmes. "She admits killing her sister? Correct?" Holmes asked.

"Correct." Lestrade replied.

"Well, we almost certainly know why," said Holmes.

What had Holmes realized?

A SECOND SEQUENCE

As I may have mentioned once or even twice, Holmes liked to set me riddles. Perhaps he wanted to see how the mind of the common man worked, compared to that great intellect of his. Or maybe he simply wanted to amuse himself by proving his own superiority. Whatever the reason, one sunny day, as we strolled through Covent Garden, he started announcing some letters. (Rather loudly, I might add). They were as follows:

H H L B B C N

Holmes's question was what letter should come next.

I was able to answer it rather quickly (if I do say so myself), but can you?

"Lestrade paid us a visit earlier. He said he was looking for you," I informed Holmes as he entered the study. "It was a bit early for a Monday morning, but it sounded urgent. Do you have any idea what that might have been about?"

"Yes. Quick case, really. Cut and dried. A man was found dead yesterday by his wife, who called the police immediately. Everyone on the premises at the time of the murder was questioned, and they all explained what they were doing.

"The usual thing: the cook was cooking; the wife was asleep; the gardener had been watering the flowerbeds; the maid greeted the postman and collected the mail; and the butler said he was cleaning the study."

"Not much to go on, is it?" I commented.

"On the contrary, Watson. It is as clear as night and day."

Who was the murderer?

THE MARRYING KIND

Holmes recently returned from a wedding that had taken him all the way up into the Lake District and, in passing, mentioned that he had met a man who had married many women but had never himself been married.

"Sounds like rather the promiscuous fellow, Holmes!" I remarked.

"Not at all. In fact, quite the reverse." said Holmes.

How so?

Holmes and I took the train down to Cardiff, and then journeyed onward in a horse-drawn cab. It wound its way torturously through the Welsh countryside, en route to our meeting with the Earl of Bute. Wind and rain lashed for some hours at the carriage, which at least kept us warm and comfortable inside.

Eventually, however, we reached the Earl's estate, parts of which had been flooded by the torrential downpour. I hopped out of the cab and landed, with my typical luck, in a large, deep puddle, leaving my lower legs entirely sodden.

Holmes, always far more observant than I, neatly avoided the puddle. Then, amused as always by my misfortune, he chose to challenge me with a riddle, saying, "You seem quite wet, Watson, so what is that you see in water but which never gets wet?"

"Really, Holmes!" I said, with exasperation.

But he got me thinking, and eventually I found the answer. What was it?

THE CRYPTIC PAINTING

A mysterious delivery arrived at 221B one day. I am all for discarding strange packages, but Holmes cannot resist investigating them.

Holmes opened the wrapping, revealing an old oil painting in a rather ornately decorated frame. Just as I had, to my own surprise, begun to admire the piece, Holmes ripped the canvas straight out and flipped it over. On the back, a message read:

HTRJ YT XY UFSHWFX YWFNS XYFYNTS FY YMWJJ NS YMJ FKYJWSTTS YMNX KWNIFD.

"Looks like gibberish," I said. "And you've destroyed the painting for that?"

"It's not gibberish, Watson. It's a Caesar cipher. Look, all the letters are shifted either left or right a constant amount within the alphabet. All you need to read it is a little concentration. Alternatively, you might yourself prefer to use a pencil and paper, and a rather more mundane method of solving."

What did it say?

SISTERLY LOVE

I can hardly claim to be anything of an expert in the field of romance, although compared to Holmes I do not fare so badly. But I certainly know very little of the legal field as it pertains to the more romantic arts. Therefore, when a question on this very topic was propelled in my general direction by a stranger at afternoon tea one day, I initially did not know what to say.

The man asked me whether it was legal for a man to marry his widow's sister. Now, I must admit that my mind quickly wandered to fill in the stranger's past, one most likely highly salacious, featuring secret love and broken families. However, this chain of somewhat fanciful thought was broken by the rather unromantic sound of "The Great Sherlock Holmes" entering the conversation, and quickly dismissing the stranger.

"No, of course not," snapped Holmes. "That would obviously not be legal, but then I am sure you already know why that is."

And why is that?

THE BEAR NECESSITIES

Holmes recently returned from one of his stranger expeditions, during which he claims to have had a dangerous encounter with a bear. (I have my doubts). Of course, Holmes survived, and even if he did encounter a bear I should think that the poor bear would have run away from his sometimes insufferable tone of self-righteous certainty. But I am betraying my own frustration that I do not always solve his riddles.

As soon as Holmes entered our study, having returned from the trip, he hit me with a riddle about the supposed bear encounter. He had been staying in a house where every side of the house had spectacular southern views, and it was while standing outside this house that he had the close encounter with the bear in question.

Then he asked me, "Watson, what type was the bear?" And what type indeed?

CHILDISH NAMES

One of the rare charming things about working with Holmes is seeing his relationship with our landlady, Mrs Hudson. She is a wonderful, elderly woman who seems to care very deeply about Holmes, despite the way he sometimes dismisses her, seemingly without a second thought.

One thing that always amuses me is watching Holmes deal with her frequently rambling conversation. He does this with more grace than he will bear for anyone else, myself certainly included, so I take this as testament to his feelings toward her.

This is especially true when Mrs Hudson starts talking about her friends, and her friends' children, and her children's friends' children. You would think that Holmes might switch his ears off during these information overloads, but it seems that the man is always paying attention.

Just this morning, Mrs Hudson was talking about children's names, and was telling Holmes how Elizabeth's mother had

four children. Apparently the first was named April, the second May, and the third was named June. I was pretty certain the fourth child must be called July, but Holmes laughed contemptuously at me when I suggested it.

Why?

Two Lords and Two Ladies

Holmes and I were preparing for a journey to the Midlands, with plans to meet with Lord Freeman and Lord Torpin.

"They are family, you know," said Holmes.

"Your family?" I asked, surprised, since Holmes had rarely mentioned any family.

"No, no. The Lords are part of the same family," he clarified.

"Ah. Brothers, is it?"

"Not exactly. You see, the men were friends throughout childhood and each took a fancy to the other's mother. It ended in marriage for both of them, too," he said.

"My goodness, if the men married each other's mother, then what might the relationship between the two sons be? Oh, what a scandalous conundrum!" I pondered, rather more excitedly than I had intended to sound.

What is the relationship between the two men?

REGINALD MUSGRAVE

A TRAY GLASS

I recently recounted a tale to Mrs Hudson about a time I went up to a barman and asked for a glass of water. I believe it to be rather an amusing story, and Mrs Hudson certainly found it so. Therefore I shall share it with you.

In any case, instead of fetching me a glass to drink as I had requested, the barman suddenly slammed a tray upon the counter with frightful force, making me jump out of my skin.

But it turned out that this was exactly what I had needed, and I thanked the gentlemen before returning to my seat with no glass to drink from after all.

I might add that I am purposefully omitting an important part of the story, so that I can pose it as a question herein: why did he do that?

Holmes often remarks that I am the sort of person that thinks only inside the box, which he in no way intends as a compliment. One day, when we were faced with an unusual mystery, Holmes made that same remark again, and I objected strongly.

Holmes dropped what he was doing, and turned to me, saying, "I shall prove you have no such skill, Watson." He took out a sheet of ordinary paper and drew three dots, like so:

Holmes then continued, "Now draw a straight line that passes directly through these three marks," handing me a pen, before clarifying, "No curves allowed!".

And he had me. I could not do it, and thought it impossible until he showed me how. What is the solution?

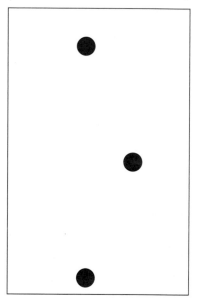

GONE TO THE DOGS

A certain case called for Holmes and myself to attend a greyhound race, to observe the actions of one Matthew Francis, a coal tycoon who had his fingers deep in the pies of the government's energy supply. Needless to say, I made sure to take part in the racing festivities. After all, the aim is to blend in.

As we walked to place our bets, Holmes asked me this: "When a dog passes the one in second position, what position will that dog now be in?"

First place, I thought. But then I wondered why Holmes was asking me. Is that correct?

THE LINKS IN THE STRAND

The word puzzle we preferred, the pyramid, was not always included in an issue of *The Strand Magazine*. On such occasions, a small blessing would be that it was replaced by an alternative word puzzle that we also found offered us some enjoyment.

This puzzle worked in a different way, with the need to find a so-called link word between two otherwise disconnected words. This word could be added to the end of one, and the start of another, to form two entirely new further words.

Let me give you an example. Say that you are given END and SHOT. You could then link them with the word EAR. How so, you may ask? Well, you would be forming ENDEAR and EARSHOT, which are both words in the English dictionary.

Now here are three for you to try yourself, all abiding by the same rules:

FORE _ _ _ _ _ IONS

KNOW _ _ _ _ _ RING

BABY _ _ _ IRE

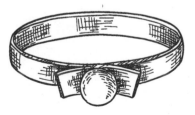

What are the link words?

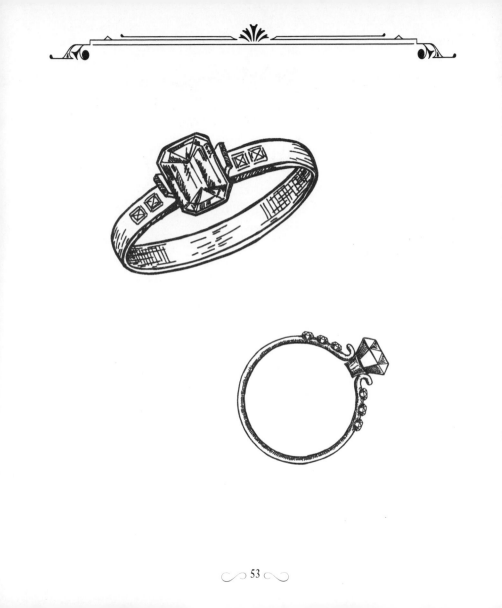

The Riddle Theory

Over the years I have noticed that one of the few people whom Holmes likes to challenge with riddles as much as me is Lestrade. I often complain of his riddles, but the truth may be that through solving so many of them I have begun to think more like Holmes. Perhaps, even, some of his genius has rubbed off on me.

Or perhaps not. It certainly does not seem to have done so on Lestrade.

Holmes does like to drop a riddle into the middle of conversation, and so it was with Lestrade one day. Following a discussion on nomenclature, Holmes casually asked Lestrade if he was "aware that there is one word that is always spelled incorrectly."

Lestrade reacted as he always did, by asking me what on earth Holmes was talking about, thus transferring the effort of solving the riddle onto me. And indeed, what was he referring to?

SOCIAL SHAKES

"A thought exercise for you, Watson!" Holmes announced to me as we were getting our shoes shined one day near Oxford Circus. This was his new term for a pointless mental challenge, and I was not keen to encourage it.

"Let's say we arrive at a dance, and we are feeling particularly friendly, so we decide that we should like to help everyone to get to know each other better," he began, somewhat improbably since I am quite sure I have never seen him dance even a single step.

"And what better way to meet someone properly than with a handshake? So, we announce our plan to ensure that all present can meet one another and be put at ease. The rule is simple: we shall have everyone shake hands only with someone who is shorter than them. So, if they encounter someone taller than them, they should not shake hands with that person.

"Now, let us say there are 20 people in the room. How many handshakes would take place? Would our plan be successful?"

LONDON ZOO ONE

A case called for a close-up examination of one of London's less common residents. Though I never fully understood the reason for this, as a fan of exotic creatures, I was only too happy to accompany Holmes to London Zoo.

After a few hours examining an elephant's leg in minute detail, Holmes turned to me and challenged me to explain "what it is that has four legs and yet can never walk?"

I thought on this for a moment before asking, "Am I likely to have seen one today?"

He answered that I had. To what did he refer?

THE LINKS
IN *THE STRAND* TWO

On those occasions when our preferred word puzzle, the pyramid, was not included in an issue of *The Strand Magazine*, we would turn to its other regular puzzle, Link Words.

This puzzle worked via the need to find a so-called link word between two otherwise disconnected words. This link word could be added to the end of one, and the start of another, to form two entirely new further words.

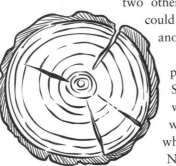

Let me repeat the example I have given you previously. Say that you are given END and SHOT. You could then link them with the word EAR. How so, you may ask? Well, you would be forming ENDEAR, and EARSHOT, which are both words in the English dictionary.

Now here are three more for you to try yourself, all abiding by the same rules:

LOG _ _ _ _ _ HOP

SUB _ _ _ _ LIGHT

REF _ _ _ _ FALL

What are the link words?

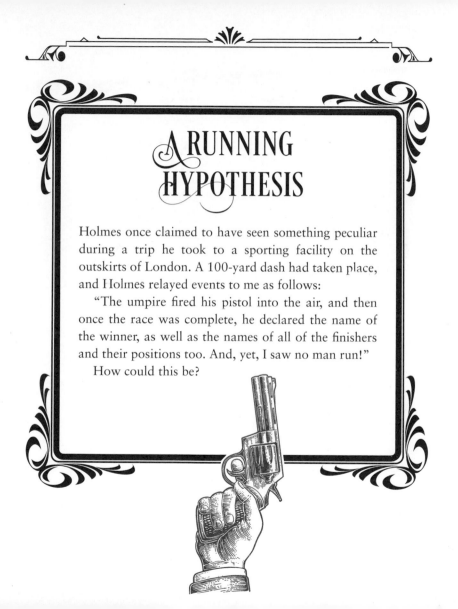

A RUNNING HYPOTHESIS

Holmes once claimed to have seen something peculiar during a trip he took to a sporting facility on the outskirts of London. A 100-yard dash had taken place, and Holmes relayed events to me as follows:

"The umpire fired his pistol into the air, and then once the race was complete, he declared the name of the winner, as well as the names of all of the finishers and their positions too. And, yet, I saw no man run!"

How could this be?

SHAKESPEARE'S WORK

"How familiar are you with Shakespeare's plays, Watson?" Holmes asked me one day during a trip to the British Library.

"I have read a few of them, and seen a fair few performed," I replied.

"But how familiar are you with them? For I have a riddle for you, but it would require an extensive knowledge of Shakespeare's plays for you to be able to consider it.

"On second thoughts, perhaps it might be too complex," he pondered, "especially as it involves a pun of sorts and I know that you are rather a literal chap."

"No, no, have at it!" I insisted, making a mental note to later refute his "literal chap" slight.

"All right, fine. Then tell me this: which Shakespearean character killed the most birds?"

A Remarkable Calculation

Holmes and I were on a train to Cambridge one day, when I was disrupted from my trance-like window-gazing by Holmes quietly chuckling to himself. I looked over to him and asked whatever the matter was. In response, he flipped his journal around in his hand so I could catch a glimpse of what he had written, showing two separate lines:

$$\text{ELEVEN} + \text{TWO}$$
$$\text{TWELVE} + \text{ONE}$$

"Remarkable, isn't it?" he said.

I was confused. "Is this not simple mathematics, Holmes? I don't see anything remarkable about it. The answer to both is thirteen, surely?"

"Yes, but what is remarkable about them both?" he replied.

It took me to the end of the train journey to work it out. What was it?

THE RIDDLE SESSION ONE

Holmes does love to pose the occasional (or, perhaps that should be frequent) riddle, but on one particular day I felt sufficiently emboldened to try some of my own on him.

Here is the one I opened with. Perhaps you would fancy trying it yourself?

"Holmes," I began, "it is time to even the riddle score! Tell me of what I speak: There is something in this world from which you can take away the whole, and yet still have some left."

Holmes replied that this sounded the most wonderful thing, but that sadly he knew it to be... well, what was the answer?

On days when nothing was afoot, and we had exhausted the puzzles contained in the relevant pages of *The Strand Magazine*, Holmes and I would sometimes devise our own brainteasers.

One we particularly liked was the letter jumble game. For this, one of us would speak a word to the other, along with a number. The other party would then have five minutes to find that given number of jumbles of the letters of the other words.

Let me give you an example, to clarify matters somewhat. Say that the word was SKATE and the number was three, then the jumbles would be STAKE, STEAK, and TAKES. All use the same letters, but in a different order, while still being legitimate words.

Some days we came up with better puzzles from others. So try the following, which was one I especially liked:

REINS. Four

Can you find all the jumbles?

A MUDDY MAN

On a recent trip to Oxford, I had been fortunate enough to pick up several first edition copies of an author I rather admired. Later, back at the apartment, I sat and read as the rain poured down outside.

My period of relaxing calm was suddenly broken by the arrival of Sherlock, who entered the room drenched with rain and covered in mud.

"The rain I understand," I commented, "but the mud perplexes me. Lunch at the farm, was it? Or did you trip getting off the carriage?"

"Very droll, Watson. In fact, I shall have you know that I fell some distance from a thirty-foot ladder at one of the new bridge constructions on the Thames," said Holmes.

"Good lord! Are you hurt?!" I exclaimed. But of course, he wasn't. Why?

THE TERRACE SPECTRUM

A tip-off had brought us to a modern housing development, where they were busy constructing long rows of terraced accommodation. We were searching for a precious jewel, which had supposedly been buried in one of the prepared foundation areas.

Our efforts ultimately proved fruitless, and as the sun began setting we found ourselves watching over the men who were building the houses.

Holmes began musing to himself, saying, "If a red house is made of red bricks, as these mid-terrace houses are, and if a brown house is made of brown bricks, as I think the end of terrace houses are, then I wonder what a green house would be built from?"

"Green bricks," I replied, wondering if such a thing existed.

Of course, I later realized what it would actually be built from. What?

A
HAIRY PROBLEM

One day, en route to meeting a duchess at Kew Gardens, I brought a hand up to brush a stray eyelash from my eye, and discovered that I had forgotten to shave that morning. Holmes helpfully commented on how he had thought I looked a little haggard today.

"Not what I need right now, Holmes," I said.

"It's funny, though, Watson. I met a man last week who shaves several times a day and yet never seems to have any less hair. How is that possible?"

"A circus performer, perhaps?" I said, more concerned with my own egregious state than whatever riddle he was spinning.

"No, no. Much less elaborate than that, Watson," he said.

What is Holmes talking about?

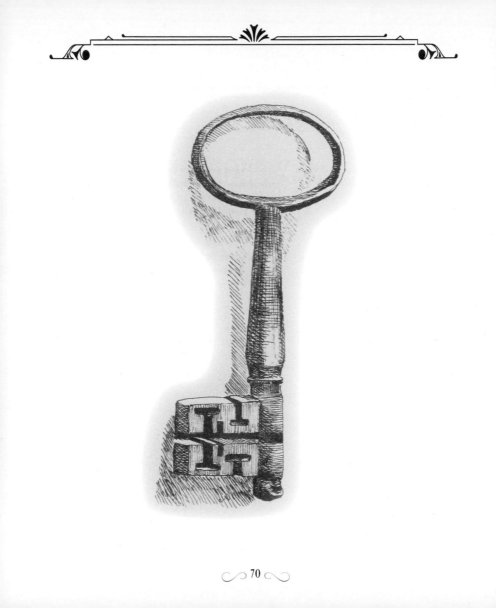

THE KEY PLACE

An old man had passed away, and I was called to the scene without Holmes. This was a rare situation, and I made it a personal mission to complete the task at hand without my good friend.

The widow of the old man told me that her late husband had hidden the key to their safe deposit box somewhere in the house. He had unfortunately found himself unable to clearly explain on his deathbed where he had hidden it. All the widow had to go on was a note that he had once written himself, lest he forget where he had put it.

The note read, "It has a tongue but cannot eat; and often walks, but never alone."

Well, finally all those years of Holmes' riddles paid off, and I am proud to report that I was able to locate the key for the woman.

Where was the object hidden?

CUBIST ARCHITECTURE

I accept that I will never fully understand the inner workings of Holmes' mind, and so when I one day entered his abode to find him building a large, cube-like piece of furniture in the middle of his study, I was less surprised than you might expect.

In such situations, I tend to avoid asking him what he is doing, lest I encourage a long lecture on some particular subject, but this did not stop him from explaining anyway.

"Watson, consider this. A cube is such a pure structure. All six faces are equal, and it flows with symmetry. And yet, if you hold a cube in your hand, consider that you can only see three of those faces at any time. How do you know that such perfect symmetry exists, until you view the far side?

"Would it not be much better if you could see straight through the cube, and view all those sides at once? Alas, I have not been able to find a perfect glass cube. And yet, I have now found a way to view all six sides of a cube without having to move either my body or the cube. I simply turn my head and there it all is."

I responded that I did not think that using mirrors was particularly clever.

"No, no, Watson. Not with mirrors. Quite another method."

What was he referring to?

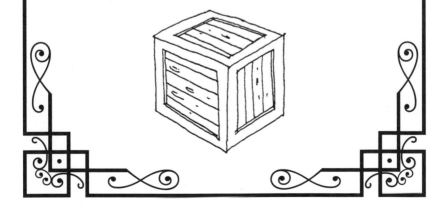

London Zoo Two

During my aforementioned trip to London Zoo with Holmes, we happened at one point to pause outside the bear exhibit. As mentioned, I really did not know what it was that Holmes was looking for at the zoo.

Holmes seemed lost in a reverie, but then he turned and asked me, "Watson, tell me this: What do you call a bear with no ear?"

I looked down at the bear in the enclosure and saw that it clearly had both ears intact. So I thought on it further, but no answer came to me. What had Holmes intended me to say?

THE HAPPY SEPARATION

One evening, after finishing a case, Holmes invited me to a game of bezique, but I declined due to existing plans. The next day, Holmes quizzed me on the event.

"It's not like you to have plans, Watson," he commented somewhat derisively. "What was the occasion?"

"Well, it was quite the event! Some acquaintances of mine, Abigail and Benjamin, who have been married for perhaps fifteen years and I have always thought were very much in love, had some news to share with me. To wit, Benjamin announced that he has filed for divorce. And Abigail is entirely delighted!"

"Sounds strange... Ah, but I see you are testing me, Watson," replied Holmes.

What was he talking about? Why was Abigail delighted?

LOST PROPERTY

When you live in a titanic city such as London, people drop things on the ground every day. Indeed, I wager that you could fill entire museums with all the trinkets that strangers unsuspectingly leave on the ground in but a single year.

Today, I observed an unusual combination. Laying at the edge of a park I observed a woolly scarf with a carrot neatly placed on top. It was not immediately clear to me why they should have been left together, but of course Holmes understood it immediately.

Why were they together?

THE CONSULTANT'S DILEMMA

A friend of mine is a much sought-after consultant, and has been offered his pick of jobs. In his most recent employ, he accepted a handsome sum of £100 per year, with the offer of regular pay rises.

He was offered two plans. One would involve his annual salary rising by 20% every year, and the other would offer an increase of 9.5% every six months. In either case, he would be paid at the end of each six-month period.

Which did he pick?

LONDON ZOO THREE

Holmes somehow filled a journal with notes while at the zoo, and in the carriage on the way back to 221B was flicking furiously through his sketches and notes, looking for I know not what.

One particular image of an animal highly amused him, since it prompted him to ask: "What has a head but cannot talk, and has a tail yet cannot walk?"

I thought back through all of the things we had seen at the zoo, but couldn't think of what it was. What did Holmes speak of?

A THIRD SEQUENCE

Rather bitten by the sequence bug, Holmes would spring them on me with no notice whatsoever, and no matter how inappropriate the situation.

During a particularly morbid visit to the undertaker, he chose that inauspicious occasion to try the following sequence on me. The aim, once again, is to divine what letter should follow next, and why.

V I B G Y O

Indeed, what does come next?

OLD AND NEW

Mrs Hudson warmly invited Holmes and myself to join her in a family gathering for the celebration of yet another grandchild. You might expect Holmes to find babies unremarkable creatures, but in actuality he is quite affectionate in their presence. As he held the child (no more than four weeks of age) in his arms, he leaned over to me and asked, with a seriousness that did not befit the question: "What is it that is never more than a month old, and yet has existed for millions of years?"

THE STRAND PYRAMID TWO

I have previously discussed the particular puzzle from *The Strand Magazine* which both Holmes and I enjoyed. I thought you might be keen to test your mental acuity again, so I present here to you the second of its type that we encountered.

As a reminder, the puzzle is built from words. The only confusion was that the words themselves were not given, but rather clues. It was up to the reader to discover the words.

To assist in this task, a particular property was noted. Each clue was solved using the same set of letters as the word before, but with the addition of one further letter. The letters could, however, then be jumbled as you pleased. It might also be worth stating that the first clue was always solved by a three-letter word, and that the pyramid was built (somewhat improbably) from the top downward.

Here is that second pyramid puzzle:

1. Droop
2. Portable holders
3. Snatches
4. River conveyances
5. Nocturnal mammals with distinctive head markings
6. Shortens

Can you solve it?

THE STRANGE SQUARE

I was reading a newspaper one day and I came across the following riddle, which I verified by tearing the paper up. It transpired that one could take these shapes from a square:

...and then rearrange them into a square with a piece left over, thus:

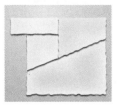

I called Holmes over to take a look at this shapely mystery, but he was surprisingly unimpressed.

"Come, Watson. Surely you are not impressed by such a simple trick. Is it not obvious what is going on here?"

What is the explanation?

THE

STRAND MAGAZINE

An Illustrated Monthly

EDITED BY

GEO. NEWNES

Vol. I.

JANUARY TO JUNE

❖❖❖

London:

BURLEIGH STREET, STRAND

1891

THE LETTER JUMBLES TWO

As I have mentioned, after we had exhausted the puzzles in *The Strand Magazine*, Holmes and I would turn to our brainteasers.

One we particularly liked was the letter jumble game. For this, one of us would speak a word to the other, along with a number. The other party would then have five minutes to find that given number of jumbles of the letters of the other words.

Let me repeat my example, to clarify matters somewhat. Say that the word was SKATE and the number was three, three, then the jumbles would be STAKE, STEAK, and TAKES. All use the same letters, but in a different order, while still being legitimate words.

Here is another of our puzzles:

RECANT. Three

Can you find all the jumbles?

THE CHEMICAL MIX-UP

We were called to an unusual case where a chemist had accidentally caused great problems due to a mishap in the laboratory. After a failure to adequately label some containers, the man had mistaken two separate vats for the same liquid, and mixed them.

To be precise, he had had two vats, each containing the same amount of liquid. One held chemical A, and the other chemical B. (The actual names escape me.) In an attempt to balance their levels, he had taken a pint of liquid from container A and poured it into the other, but then seen that their levels now differed and poured a pint of liquid back from container B to the other. Once again their levels were now equal.

The chemist now wondered if either chemical could still be sold, given that it was mixed with another substance. Each substance was inert, so no chemical reactions had taken place; the two liquids were simply mixed.

Naturally he wishes to start with the container that is most pure, so which container, A or B, contains the purest mixture?

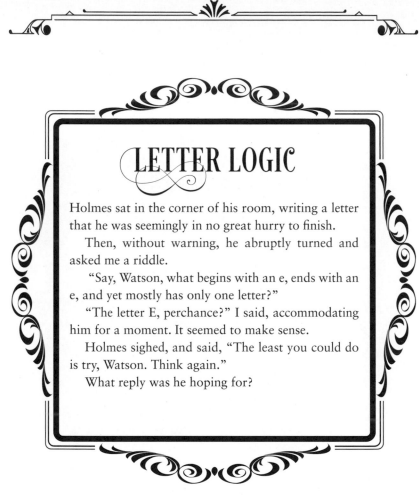

LETTER LOGIC

Holmes sat in the corner of his room, writing a letter that he was seemingly in no great hurry to finish.

Then, without warning, he abruptly turned and asked me a riddle.

"Say, Watson, what begins with an e, ends with an e, and yet mostly has only one letter?"

"The letter E, perchance?" I said, accommodating him for a moment. It seemed to make sense.

Holmes sighed, and said, "The least you could do is try, Watson. Think again."

What reply was he hoping for?

THE CLOCK RIDDLE ONE

I was once sitting comfortably by Holmes' fireplace when I heard the tolling of a grandfather clock. I was immediately struck by the sound, as it sounded so like the one in my own apartment. I stood up to take a closer look, and of course quickly discovered that Holmes had somehow misappropriated it from my chambers.

"Holmes!" I called. He eventually entered the room. "My grandfather clock! What is it doing here? And how did you get it all this way?" I demanded.

"Hush now, dear boy. And if you're willing to ponder aloud for a moment, answer me this: What is used by other people more than you, even if it is yours?" Holmes asked.

"My grandfather clock, self-evidently!" I protested.

"No, no. It is a riddle, Watson."

What was he talking about?

THE LINKS IN *THE STRAND* THREE

When our preferred word puzzle, the pyramid, was not in an issue of *The Strand Magazine*, we would turn to its other regular puzzle, Link Words.

This puzzle involved finding a link word between two otherwise disconnected words. This word could be added to the end of one, and the start of another, to form two entirely new further words.

Let me repeat the example given previously. Say that you are given END and SHOT. You could link them with the word EAR. How so, you may ask? Well, you would be forming ENDEAR, and EARSHOT, which are both words in the dictionary.

Now here are three more for you to try yourself, all abiding by the same rules:

OVERT _ _ _ _ ELF

SKIN _ _ _ _ _ ROPE

DISCUS _ _ _ _ LED

What are the link words?

TIMING TROUBLE

I once entered 221B during a period of time when we had a moratorium on new cases. In times like these it can feel like I am intruding, and indeed on this occasion I found Holmes sitting cross-legged on the floor, surrounded by blankets on every wall.

"Before you ask, Watson" Holmes began, "I have freed us from all mechanical ticking noises. So very loud; I could not bear to think with them around. Not today, Watson."

"And where precisely have you put my grandfather clock, Holmes?" I asked, half-worried that he had done something rash. "Is this some absurd hangover remedy? Have you been drinking?" I was yet to take my grandfather clock back home, after he had purloined it.

"Never mind that now, Watson. I have turned to the sands for all my timekeeping," he replied, presenting two sandglasses. "One of these has a five-minute duration, and the other has a seven-minute duration."

"But what if you wanted to time something for longer, and not a multiple of five or seven minutes?" I asked. "What if you wanted to time something for, say, nine minutes? What then?"

"No problem! You can easily time nine minutes," he responded. How?

THE RIDDLE SESSION TWO

During a particular session in which I had just asked Holmes a riddle of my own devising, Holmes had not dismissed me out of hand, so I felt I would keep striking while the metaphorical iron was hot.

I moved on with a second riddle.

"Holmes, here is another.

"There is something in this world..."

Holmes interjected that it sounded like I was very much about to ask him a riddle he had heard before.

I persevered, continuing, "...that always ends up with just a nose, whenever it loses an eye. What is that thing?"

What indeed?

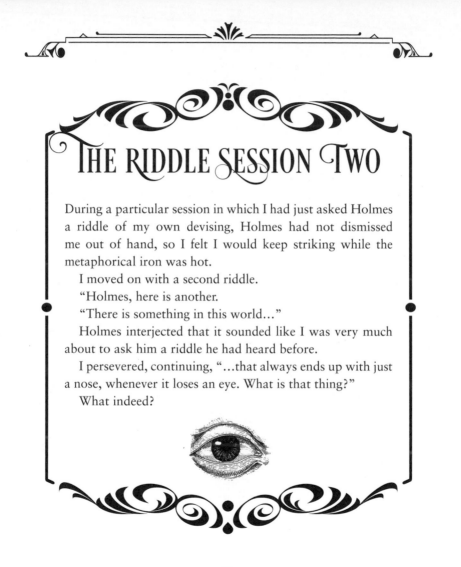

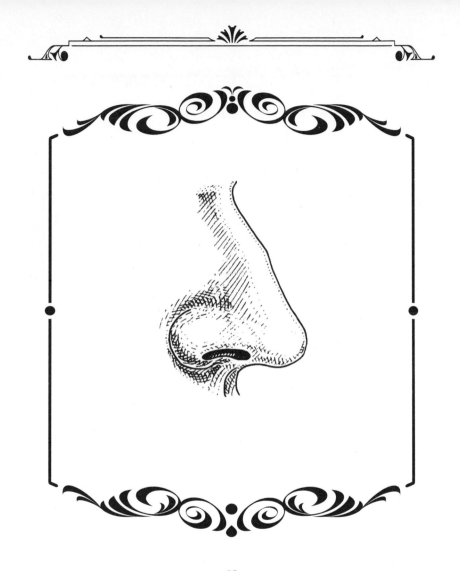

THE FRENCH MATHEMATICIAN

Holmes and I were visiting a French mathematician by the name of Marie Lecloud, to offer some much-needed assistance in a case.

Now, as you know, Holmes is so infuriatingly right most of the time that any attempt to point out a weakness is sure to be met with a metaphorical slap across the jaw as he proceeds to prove you wrong. This was a particularly enjoyable encounter for me, therefore, since Mme Lecloud was able to best Holmes, at least briefly.

"That mysterious letter sequence that you failed to identify, several cases ago, was so desperately obvious that I began to doubt your genius, Holmes," she joked, perhaps not realizing how dangerous such a thing could prove. "It should have been immediately apparent for what it was."

She was referring to a sequence scrawled on a note that had later appeared in the press. It read:

U D T Q C S S H N D.

"Indeed, Madame?" Holmes queried in clipped tones. "I am not surprised you knew it, although I must confess it took me some hours to discover its meaning."

What does the sequence refer to?

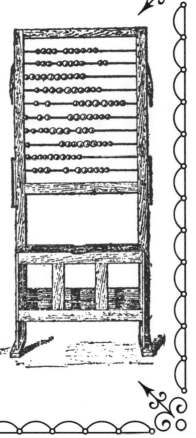

THE CLOCK RIDDLE TWO

I decided to take back home the grandfather clock that Holmes had previously taken from me, and since it was so complex to move I took the chance to have some of the damage it had accumulated fixed.

After it returned from the repair shop, however, there seemed to be a problem that had not previously existed. To be precise, the other day I checked the time and thought it rather odd. My pocket watch told me it was 7:20, and yet the grandfather clock read 4:35. Of course, I thought it must be running slow and made a note to correct it. But, later that same day, I checked again, and this time my grandfather clock told me it was 11:45 when in reality it was 9:00.

Can you work out what has gone wrong?

THE WATER PUZZLE

Holmes and myself had a further encounter with Mme Lecloud, the renowned mathematician. We had been hired by a client to calculate the volume of water in a large enclosed system, but it was so complex that Sherlock felt that a mathematical brain might be of some assist.

Bleeding the water from the system to measure it in its entirety was not acceptable, and the system was intricate enough that taking meticulous measurements of the pipes, as well as other chambers in the system, was impractical in the extreme. These would not in any case necessarily represent the volume of water, since it might not fill the chambers.

What was the method that Holmes and Marie devised to estimate the total volume of water in the system?

THE LATE TRAIN

Holmes and I were on our way to an engagement and, as seems so often to be the case, the train was running late. This sometimes agitates Holmes greatly, perhaps because it reminds him that some things are beyond even his control.

"Fifteen minutes late, Holmes!" I complained. "This wretched train is never coming."

"I suppose it shall arrive eventually." he responded, before continuing, "but I put it to you: There is something that is always coming and yet never arrives. What is it?"

And what, indeed, is it?

RUNNING LOGIC

Holmes can move quickly when he needs to, and one particular day I saw him chase down and apprehend a thief who I felt sure was about to escape.

"You should run in competitions!" I remarked later, sitting with Holmes in the kitchen at 221B.

"And waste time when I could be doing something actually useful?" he reproached me.

"Well, if I had the physical capabilities, I should certainly think of competing," I said.

"My preferred running is of the mental kind. But still, they can be combined, I suppose, so try this. Imagine you are running the 200 yards, and you overtake the runner in last place. What position would they be in now?"

It seemed obvious that they must now be in last place instead, but what was I missing?

THE STRAND PYRAMID THREE

As you will note, I have previously discussed the particular puzzle from *The Strand Magazine* which both Holmes and I enjoyed. I thought you might be keen to test your mental acuity again, so I present here to you the third of its type that we encountered.

As a reminder, the puzzle is built from words. The only confusion, however, was that the words themselves were not given, but rather clues. It was up to the reader to discover the words.

To assist in this task, a particular property was noted. Each clue was solved using the same set of letters as the word before, but with the addition of one further letter. The letters could, however, then be jumbled as you pleased. It might also be worth stating that the first clue was always solved by a three-letter word, and that the pyramid was built (somewhat improbably) from the top downward.

Here is that third pyramid puzzle:
1. Fishing stick
2. Highway
3. Transmitter
4. Make someone a priest
5. Progress
6. Extinct beast
Can you solve it?

THE MUSIC MAN

"Tell me, have you ever played any instruments, Watson?" Holmes asked me one day, while playing his violin.

"It is not something I have engaged in with any sincerity, which I admit with some regret," I responded.

"And if you could right this musical wrong, and learn to play an instrument, then what would you choose?" he queried.

"Well, I enjoy the sound of the harp, but it is far too large to carry. So something portable, I suppose."

"Aha! Watson, I know just the thing! But I must warn you, it is an instrument that you can neither see nor touch. And yet it is highly portable, I assure you. Indeed, I daresay you may have even made music with it before, although I must admit no memory of hearing this myself."

What instrument did Holmes refer to?

THE BARRACKS BURGLARY

During a visit to my old army barracks one day, I met up with some former colleagues to reminisce and to reacquaint my memories of the location with the place itself.

Now it just so happened that a burglary had taken place in one of the quarters mere hours before my arrival. Upon hearing about my presence, I was naturally called by the presiding officer to attend the investigation. I admit that I was a little nervous to be operating without Holmes, but I was determined to sniff out the answer nevertheless.

When I arrived on the scene, I was presented with three suspects, who were instructed to give me their alibis:

The first assured me that he was in the stables, cleaning out horse manure.

The second informed me that someone had flown the St George's Flag upside down and he was busy re-hoisting the flag in the correct orientation on the flagpole during the incident.

The third recounted that he was in the laundry room, but he could not say what he had been washing.

I thought on this for a moment, then pronounced one of the suspects guilty. Later, I am told, the man confessed.

Who was the guilty party?

One day a visitor attended us at 221B, bringing a letter they had received from a friend which contained a cryptic message they could make neither head nor tail of.

It read as follows:

> *My Dearest Friend,*
> *I trust you have received this letter in good time, for I have found myself obsessed by the contents of a mathematical equation that only you will be able to help me solve.*
> *Before I lose hold of my senses, can you help me with the problem I set out below?*

> *Yours,*
> *A.*

Holmes stared at the page for a moment, but then dismissed the matter as too trivial for his great intellect to consider. I thought he had been bested, but it turned out he knew perfectly well what the equation meant.

What was the secret of the letter?

THE COIN CONUNDRUM

Occasionally a client will pay us with a pile of coins, and after one such case Holmes and I entered a tavern, preparing ourselves for the journey back to Baker Street.

Sitting at a table, Holmes placed ten of the coins in two rows on the table, like so:

"Watson, I have a challenge for you! See if you can arrange these coins into five straight rows, whereby each row is made up of precisely four coins. What's more, you may move only four coins from their current position."

How did I solve it?

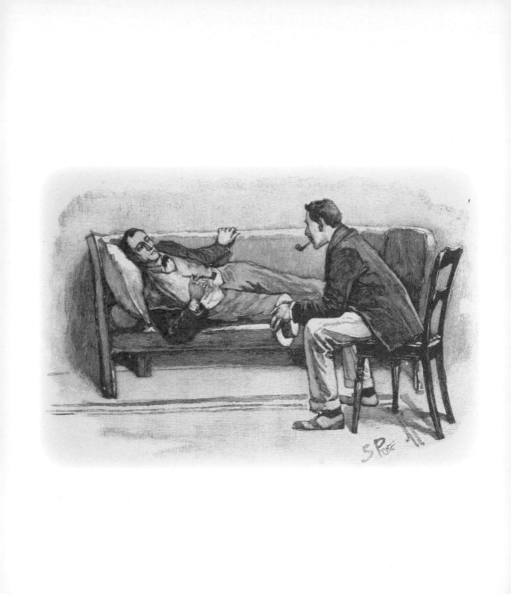

A RETURN FROM ROME

One evening, on a long boat trip back from Rome to deal with a particularly significant continental case, I plucked up the courage to ask Holmes a riddle of my own making.

I approached him in the lounge, where I found him feeding himself grapes on a chaise longue.

I began, "There is a family where the eldest daughter is eleven, and the son is half her age. Their cousin is..."

"So the son is six," Holmes interrupted.

"Pardon me? No, Holmes, half of eleven is never six."

"Well it has just occurred to me that it can be, and you will hardly be able to argue with me when you see how. How may I halve eleven to make six?"

How indeed could he?

THE WORD GAME

"Watson, I have found another game for you!" said Holmes, holding up a page from a particular magazine of which he was fond.

"Perhaps we should be directing our creative efforts toward our case?" I replied.

"This is a letter removal puzzle," he continued, ignoring me. "Each line contains the same word, except that with each progressive line a letter has been removed. The other letters are not changed or rearranged in any way. For example, you might move from GOLD to GOD simply by removing the L.

"It comes in the form of a poem of sorts, with one word blanked out per line. Your job is to find those missing words. And I suppose I should add that the first contains nine letters.

"Here, take a look," he said, throwing the page over to me. "You must find the words."

A figure, striking, _____(9) me,
Dark like_____(8)'s shadows be,
From _____(7) darkness, threatening,
Eyes like saucers, hair like_____(6),
Sharpened teeth and pointed_____(5),
Its grumbling growl, I hear it _____(4),
Perchance a_____(3) to face from high,
_____(2) times of fight or flight to sky:
_____(1) alone must face the beast.

THE ROYAL DIVISION

A member of the Royal Family came to Holmes and myself with an unusual request. I am not at liberty to reveal who it was, but I can reveal that he wanted our help to settle a land ownership issue. Normally we would deny a request like this, but we made an exception in this case (although not without some initial protest from Holmes).

This particular member of the Royal Family had come into ownership of a perfectly square portion of the Crown Estate and, to simplify matters of succession, decided to gift his four children equal parts of his land.

Our royal client wished to keep a quarter of the land for himself and gift the remaining three quarters equally to his four children. The plot of the estate is shown below, with the reserved quarter marked out already:

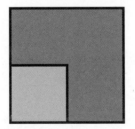

To keep their affairs as simple and conflict-free as possible, he also asked that the division divide the remaining land into parcels of land that were all identical in shapes.

How did Holmes propose he do this?

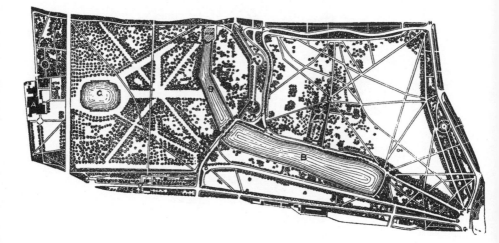

THE RAIN GAME

I need not tell you how changeable the weather can be in this country, and indeed today as I write this is no exception. But in any case, I was recently with Holmes in Kensington when we were caught in a terrible downpour.

"I am fully expecting actual cats and dogs to start falling!" I yelled through the heavy cacophony of rain on cobble, adding, "I shall never be dry again."

"The rain is certainly enjoying falling down today," responded Holmes, "but do not forget that as the rain falls down something else goes up."

What was he talking about?

I recently spent a week in Brighton, in an attempt to escape the smog of London. Unfortunately, I found myself trapped inside by rain, and spent much of the week in a hotel room.

From my hotel window, I watched as the downpour battered the beach, and wondered at the brave souls attempting to walk their dogs along the shoreline despite the monstrous waves.

Watching those wet souls did, however, bring to mind a riddle that I kept ready for the next time Holmes and I were together.

Here it is: "What gets left behind whenever it is taken?"

THE CALENDAR CLUB

"When are we meeting with the French ambassador?" I asked Holmes, scanning a calendar for an appointment that I could not discern. I rather suspects Holmes had deliberately forgotten to make it.

"Oh, the Gregorian calendar is far too complex." he responded, preposterously. "Have you ever heard of the 'International Fixed Calendar'?"

"Holmes, just pick a date and I shall make the arrangements," I said, mildly frustrated by his digressions.

"Fine. I shall. But only if you can tell me what occurs once in January, once in February, and then does not occur again until June, July and August?"

What was he referring to?

THE FOREST PARK

We had tracked a killer to a certain forest, having heard from a witness who saw them flee into the treeline of the wilderness. While waiting for the Scotland Yard force to arrive, Holmes and I ventured into the woods to search for clues to their precise location.

The sea of trees seemed endless, and Holmes was unusually circumspect. Eventually I commented that I felt sure we must be almost three-quarters of the way into the forest.

"Impossible!" barked Holmes, dismissing me.

"I am fairly sure that—", I tried to respond, but he cut me off again.

"You can never travel more than half of the way into a forest".

Why did he say this?

THE LETTER JUMBLES THREE

As I have mentioned, after we had exhausted the puzzles in *The Strand Magazine*, Holmes and I would turn to our brainteasers.

One we particularly liked was the letter jumble game. For this, one of us would speak a word to the other, along with a number. The other party would then have five minutes to find that given number of jumbles of the letters of the other words.

Let me repeat my example, to clarify matters somewhat. Say that the word was SKATE and the number was three, then the jumbles would be STAKE, STEAK, and TAKES. All use the same letters, but in a different order, while still being legitimate words.

Here is another of our puzzles:

PALEST. Five

Can you find all the jumbles?

A HIDDEN MESSAGE

Holmes receives rather a large amount of unbidden communications, often asking for help in cracking a coded message that the recipient has received from a friend or admirer. Sometimes we ourselves receive such coded messages too.

Here is one such message. Can you work out what it says?

Hotel Londinium, 25th September
Dear Mr Holmes,

I hate to echo the many requests for autographs you no doubt receive, but I am stuck here in Lima and collecting them is one of my few amusements, a hobby acquired from my papa. Perhaps you will be able to help me acquire one?

My husband Mike tells me that I should keep this brief, so I will simply echo my request: if you can send such a trinket, please let me know.

Yours,
Jane Holbeck

I must admit that I felt the message told me almost nothing, but Holmes reacted more strongly than I expected. What had he found hidden within it?

OFF TO THE RACES

Holmes and I are not treated to brain-twisting mysteries every day. Although this can sometimes represent a welcome respite from the moral stench of this country's nefarious underworld, the somewhat less welcome result is a lack of an excuse to avoid dealing with the overflowing pile of mundane requests for help which we are otherwise happy to ignore.

One such request that has stuck with me is a case whereby two brothers found themselves arguing over a conditional will, following the death of their father. During his lifetime he had loved to set one against the other via a series of challenges, and in his will he had chosen to do the same.

Both brothers were jockeys, so the father's will offered one last challenge, requiring that they should race for his inheritance. Now normally this would be of little interest, but in this case the stipulation was that the brother whose horse loses the race would receive the entirety of their father's money.

The brothers feared this would result in a ridiculously slow race that would go on forever, so, for advice on how best to settle things, they paid Holmes and myself a visit at 221B Baker Street for some advice. Holmes, of course, had the answer at once.

The next day the brothers took the horses to the track and raced their horses at full speed to try to win their father's money.

What had Holmes advised them to do?

THE CODED COMMUNICATION

"Take a look at this," I said, handing Holmes an anonymous message that had just arrived. At the time, he was lying on the ground in his sitting room, in the midst of what he claimed was an experiment. What it entailed, I could not say.

"It's very rude of you, Watson, to not knock before coming in," he said, ignoring the note that I proffered.

"It is less than five minutes since I left the room, Holmes," I rejoined.

"And of what relevance is that?" he replied.

"Complete relevance. I merely popped out and then back in. In such cases, convention surely states that I need not knock." But this then led me to muse, "If I had been absent for ten minutes, or certainly more, then I do suppose a knock would have been more appropriate."

This trivial conversation continued for some minutes, but eventually Holmes did deign to scan the message, which had been

written in code by an anonymous informant.
It read as follows:

UBGRALYR OTINHGT
XOOFDR TSERTE
OMIRRAYT

Holmes stared at me gravely. "We had better warn Lestrade."

What did the message read?

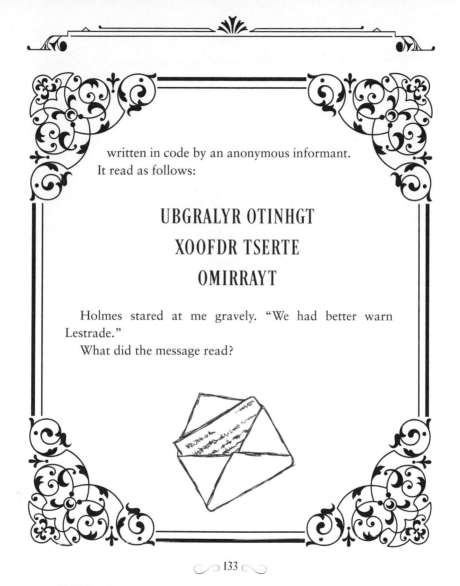

A FOURTH SEQUENCE

Holmes was not a religious man, so perhaps I should not have been surprised when, on a visit to St Paul's Cathedral, he chose that particular moment to set me another of his infernal sequence riddles.

The aim, once again, was to work out which letter should come next in the sequence.

On this particular occasion, the sequence was as follows:

G E L N D J J

Perhaps the situation inspired Holmes, but I was surprised by this choice. What was the answer?

AN INEXACT SCIENCE

Holmes and I were called to the laboratory of one Henry Lalziggen, a renowned chemist from Germany who happened currently to reside near a notorious asylum situated in North Berkshire. The man had been kidnapped and little had been found in the way of clues to help the police locate him. Suspicion naturally fell on a certain resident of the asylum who had recently escaped but then been recaptured.

Another suspect was his young assistant, barely more than a boy, who warned us that Lalziggen had recently been targeted by extremists over his development of certain theories that were felt to be anathema to the Established Church.

Reading through his mail revealed that he had also been under pressure from various different groups, including a scientist and a local love rival who had threatened him for making overtures to a particular woman.

In his laboratory, underneath a towering Periodic Table poster, lay a large variety of test tubes, arranged in a most torturous pattern that I felt sure was important. It almost seemed as if they made the numbers 5, 8, and 39.

Who did Holmes recommend the police arrest?

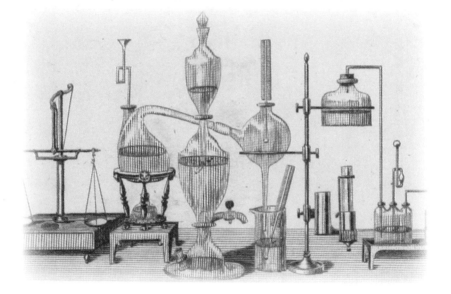

GOING UNDERGROUND

A particularly unpleasant case led myself and Holmes down a labyrinth of sewage tunnels beneath London. We were unable to bring oil lamps with us due to the gases, but the occasional grating allowed in just enough light to stop the place being hopelessly dark. This was a godsend since the rest of our senses were becoming paralyzed by the intense smell of London's sewage.

"This is hopeless, Holmes," I said. "We need some light down here."

"Feel around for the walls, Watson. Use your legs if you must. And to distract your mind from the task at

hand, consider this: if you had an oil lamp, a methanol-soaked torch, a bundle of newspapers, and only one match, which of these would you light first? Assuming it were safe to do so, of course."

THE URBAN CLIFF

Only a few weeks ago, Holmes and I attended an unfortunate case in Mayfair wherein a man had fallen from the fourth-floor window of a building and had, unsurprisingly, perished on encountering the cobbles below. Upon our arrival, the police were quick to inform us that no part of his apartment had been tampered with, and that no one other than the police had been allowed in or out of the premises since their arrival.

The police had spoken to nearby residents, who reported that the man had been deeply troubled, so the police strongly suspected suicide as the cause of his death.

As the police finished explaining the case, a caretaker arrived with a key to the apartment, so we were able to head up to examine the room. Before we did, however, Holmes, who had been looking up at the building, confidently announced, "Not a suicide, but a murder."

We were all perplexed. "Watch carefully," said Holmes. He went up to the apartment, and we saw him gingerly open the window above the body using gloves, before waving down to us to beckon us up.

Why did Holmes believe it was murder?

A recent letter that arrived read as follows:

> *If I may be so bold,*
> *Let me say how much it means to*
> *one such as I that you have chosen*
> *very much to remain in London.*
> *Every day you are here we benefit.*
>
> *Your presence makes us safer, not*
> *only through solving, but also the*
> *underworld's fear of you.*
>
> *Sandra Grey*

Holmes laughed when he read it, and it took me a moment to work out what he had seen, but I must admit that I then found it very funny too.

What message did it conceal?

A GHOSTLY ENCOUNTER

You will surely be aware of Dame Katherine Devallier and her operatic talents. One day, therefore, it was something of a thrill when she attended our office. Once seated with a cup of tea (with two sugars "for my nerves"), she surprised us by telling an unlikely story of a ghostly visitation.

The famous Dame had a twin sister, but she had sadly passed away nearly three years previously. But then, one windy night, Dame Devallier was roused from her sleep by a strange noise, and rose to catch sight of an apparition of her long-deceased sister staring back at her from above her dressing table. She jumped out of bed and lit a candle, but the spirit was gone.

She seemed entirely convinced that either her sibling had returned to her in spirit form, or she had faked her death and returned to spy on her. I was doubtful, of course, although who is to say how the spirits may choose to manifest?

Holmes, however, was quick to dismiss her, saying that he could tackle cases of a corporeal nature only.

I was surprised by this, but Holmes explained the mystery by saying, "Put it this way, Watson. Imagine that I make two people out of one. What am I?"

THE SINGING DETECTIVE

The Goat's Hoof is a particularly fine drinking establishment that I very much recommend if ever you find yourself near to the Southampton docks. I last visited it while accompanying Holmes on a certain venture that would take us to Amsterdam by ship. Needing to make some effort to blend in with the local crowd, purely in the interests of the job, we spent some hours at the Goat's Hoof, sampling a range of their world ales.

Though he later claimed it was all part of his character research, Holmes became rather more inebriated than you might expect. I say this because in his day-to-day life he is not one for singing or making a mockery of himself. On the other hand, he does love to talk. Perhaps that is why he challenged a Scottish seaman to a bet.

"I bet you a drink—" Holmes began. Then he looked at me and my half-empty glass, and back to the Scotsman. "Ah! ... two drinks, that I know and could sing you a popular song with your name on it, my friend. Whatever that name may be!"

"Holmes, you could not possibly know sufficient songs." I warned him.

The Scotsman smiled a toothy grin, and announced his name: "Lachlan MacKinnon. And I had better know the song!"

I began to laugh nervously, since Holmes had picked a man with such a difficult and unusual name. But then Holmes began to sing, and before I knew it we had two beers in front of us, having won the bet.

To those who were not present, what song did he sing?

THE FINAL SEQUENCE

All good things must come to an end, and luckily many bad things too. A case in point was Holmes's obsession with setting me sequences to which he challenged me to divine the next element.

Having tested my sequencing mettle on four prior occasions, I am glad to report that the last of these tests came a year or so ago. In the time since, there have been none, so I am hopeful that this is the last of this particularly frustrating type of teaser.

I am sure, nonetheless, that you will be interested to share it with me. It was as follows:

K P C O F G

Luckily my background gave me a better chance than some at this. The question, as ever, is what should come next?

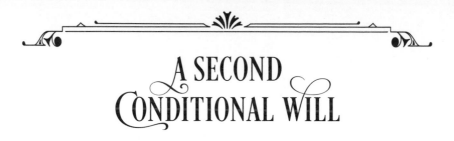

A SECOND CONDITIONAL WILL

I may have complained in the past about dealing with inheritance, but I am so entranced by the very notion of the conditional will that I always pay them attention whenever they cross my path. If you are not familiar, or should wish to provide for your friends and family in the same way after your own death, a conditional will is as the name suggests; it is a will that will be effective only in the case that a certain condition, or conditions are met.

Now, most of the time, the deceased's requests are rather benign. But the tricksters among us might make their relatives dance for their inheritance, and on this occasion there seemed to be very little motive.

A young man came to us looking for advice. His father had left an absurd will that pitted him against his two brothers for the entirety of the family fortune. In this will, the late father had provided each son with a sixpence and informed them that "whomever may entirely fill our moderately sized living room using items purchased only with the coins here provided shall lay claim to my final prize." Benjamin's brothers had attempted to purchase hay and feathered pillows to fill the space, but neither could purchase sufficient items to complete the challenge.

The remaining son, who sat across from me, begged us for a solution. Luckily for him, he was not in much competition for Holmes' attention at the time, and so the great man leaned forward and gave the young man an

answer. That young man then went out and bought two everyday items, as Holmes had instructed, and proceeded to win the inheritance.

What had Holmes suggested he purchase?

RUNNING AROUND

One evening last winter, I joined Holmes in his lounge, both to make use of his well-stocked fireplace and to corroborate certain details of an investigation that I was then writing up from my journals.

Holmes sat across from me, seemingly engrossed in a large and solid-looking book clearly entitled on the spine: HOW TO JOG. This struck me as strange since, while Holmes had a remarkable turn of speed when he needed it, I couldn't fathom why he should read upon the theory of such activity.

"Surely you already know how to jog, Holmes?" I queried.

"Come now, Watson. Of what do you speak? Why should I be learning to jog?"

I gestured to the large text in his hands. He looked at me, and then laughed somewhat derisively, saying: "I can assure you, I am not reading about jogging."

I looked at the book more closely, and realized that the binding looked familiar. I then saw that it was one of several similarly bound books on his shelves.

What was the book about?

THE CODED LETTER

We receive so many coded letters that I sometimes think Holmes must be the world's pre-eminent expert. Certainly he must be one of our foremost crackers.

This coded message arrived the other day. Here it is, in its brief entirety:

Make sure you come with all due Haste to meet the prince Regent's female friend, who is staying briefly in our town, near a certain location. Park your cab outside the building and come into the Centre.

Can you work out what it said?

Holmes had tolerated two riddles from me on a particular afternoon, so I pushed my luck and went for a hat trick, hoping that at least one would catch him out.

"Holmes, here is another. The final one, I promise.

"For which six-letter word can you remove half of the letters, and yet have only one left? It sounds impossible, but I assure you it can be done!"

Holmes snorted. "Indeed it can, Watson. Is this really a riddle or are you giving me the solution as you say it?"

What was the answer?

THE CLUB CODE

One evening I accompanied Holmes through the streets of London under the false assumption (which I think he gave me simply for his own amusement) that we were going shopping for top hats. I eventually discovered his deception when I realized that no self-respecting hat shop would be open so late in the evening. On top of that, it became clear that we were on the trail of a certain Bradley T. Warren, a distributor of dynamite who had recently been awarded a contract as part of the construction of a new underground railway.

The hunt for our quarry led us to an underground casino. This particular establishment required a password for entry, in order to deter unwanted (and accidental) guests. The methodology changed daily, so we hid in earshot of the door and waited for some patrons to arrive.

Sure enough, a member soon arrived and knocked on the door. The doorman swung open a shutter and announced: Twelve. The member responded Six, and was led inside.

A second club member knocked on the door. Six, said the doorman this time. The member replied Three, and in he went.

Finally, a third person walked up to the door. The doorman boomed Ten, and the man responded Five, but was denied entry. We then heard him muttering that he should have replied with Three.

This was enough for Holmes, and soon enough we gained admittance. How did the code work?

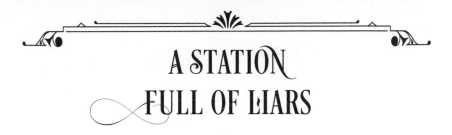

A STATION
FULL OF LIARS

Lestrade summoned us to the station after attempting to squeeze new information from a set of stones. I speak metaphorically, of course. It was a minor gang he had arrested, and it seemed to be imploding before our very eyes. Again, I speak metaphorically.

"I feel that our sting operation may have disbanded the Cranberry Bandits once and for all. They appear to have turned against each other," Lestrade said, clearly very tired.

Holmes waited for him to say more.

Lestrade continued, "Abigail here says that another member of their troupe, James, always lies. Meanwhile, James has told us that a different member of the group, Gemma, always lies."

"And what does Gemma say?" I asked.

"Gemma said that both Abigail and James always lie.

"So, who's the weak chain? Who's the one telling the truth?"

If you assume that two of them are lying, and one is telling the truth, then which is the truth-teller?

THE STRAND
PYRAMID FOUR

Here is another of that particular puzzle from *The Strand Magazine* which both Holmes and I enjoyed. I thought you might be keen to test your mental acuity again, so I present here to you the fourth of its type that we encountered.

As a reminder, the puzzle is built from words. The only confusion, however, was that the words themselves were not given, but rather clues. It was up to the reader to discover the words.

To assist in this task, a particular property was noted. Each clue was solved using the same set of letters as the word before, but with the addition of one further letter. The letters could, however, then be jumbled as you pleased. It might also be worth stating that the first clue was always solved by a three-letter word, and that the pyramid was built (somewhat improbably) from the top downwards.

Here is that fourth pyramid puzzle:

1. 24-hour period
2. Distance unit
3. Prepared
4. Very much
5. Consisting of multiple strata
6. Thought about again, as in one's mind

Can you solve it?

SECOND EDITION.

SIX PENCE

THE STRAND MAGAZINE

BURLEIGH STREET

359

EDITED by Geo: Newnes

OFFICES

Nº 7 VOL. 2

JULY 1891

AN·ILLUSTRATED·MONTHLY

THE STAMP COLLECTION

A few months ago, Holmes and I found ourselves concerned that our letters were being intercepted and read before arriving at their various destinations. We therefore decided to test our hypothesis.

We drafted three letters to be sent to three different destinations, all sent at the same time with the same stamp class, and asked our recipients to record the date on which the letter arrived. On one envelope, we listed 221B as the return address, and the other two were given a seemingly random one in order, we hoped, to avoid interception.

The Royal Mail collection time crept up on us, and due to the date-sensitive nature of the letters we found ourselves in a hurry to get them sent off. In this haste, I accidentally knocked a box of stamps behind Holmes' desk, and when I reached under for them I could grasp only one at a time. What's more, I was unable to see each stamp's value until I had pulled it out and moved it back into the light on top of the desk.

There had originally been a mix of 1d stamps, 2d stamps, and 3d stamps in the box. How many stamps would I need to pull out from under the desk until I could be sure of having three of the same value?

AN OPEN FIELD

A recent case led to a long hike through the rolling countryside of England, accompanying Sherlock to a remote manor house. The country had been battered by strong winds, and on our way through the heathlands we came across many a felled plant. I am not averse to a spot of weather, but as we approached the top of a hill a virtual gale was blowing, and we noticed that the signpost that we should have expected to help guide us had fallen over. In fact, it had been completely uprooted by the wind and thrown a

good five yards away from where it usually stood. The place we were going was clearly not buried somewhere beneath the ground, as suggested by the direction in which the arrow now pointed, and the town whence we had come was not oriented high above the clouds.

At this point in our journey there were no towns in sight, but we were able to reorient the signpost and carry on our way in the correct direction.

How did we know which way to go?

TENNIS TRICKERY

Given everything I have written about Holmes and myself, it might seem silly to ask you to picture the two of us in our tennis whites. But the truth of it is that in the summer months we have once or twice managed to contest over a net with those age-old weapons of rackets and ball.

Even with my injuries, I can still play a fair game. And, as you may have inferred, Holmes' ability to play me, from a psychological perspective, is second to none. Luckily, however, he is not always so coordinated that his plan of attack matches his footwork. So, when we play, the game truly is afoot!

During one such game I recall that we were rallying the ball between the two of us before a match, and needed a way to choose the starting server. For whatever reason, the fancy took me that I should take the ball and make a mark on the surface, then throw it up into the air. Whomever the mark pointed to would then be the man to serve. When it finally settled on the ground, the mark was facing Holmes. I tossed it over the netting to him.

However, I saw him eyeing up to ball very intently by the time I had readied myself. "Holmes? Your service!" I called.

"Interesting, though" he said. "If I were to add two further marks to this ball in two places, both chosen quite at random, what are the chances that all three marks will be on the same half of the ball?"

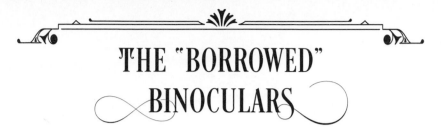

THE "BORROWED" BINOCULARS

I was rifling through one of the desks in Holmes' apartment since he had just asked me to fetch him a letter opener. Deep within the drawer, however, I discovered a set of my own binoculars that I had thought lost forever. I was quite sure that I had never brought them over to 221B.

"Holmes!" I said, storming into his room.

"Ah, excellent, you have found it," he said, holding out his hands. When I did not give him anything to grasp, he said, "But where is the letter opener?"

I presented the binoculars. "Holmes. How did these end up in your desk?" I asked, impatiently.

"Watson, surely it is self-evident. I borrowed them. I needed to see at the street level without being spotted."

I sighed, before responding, "Were you never taught to ask in order to borrow something, Holmes? Remember that you catch thieves; you ought not to be one yourself."

"Is it really a theft if it is not discovered? And besides, that reminds, me: What can be returned without being borrowed?"

I realized he had asked me another riddle even while defending himself, and of course it did succeed in distracting me from my ire. What was the answer?

THE HORSE FARM

"How was the horse wrangler?" I asked one day. "Did he have any useful information?"

Holmes responded: "No, but I accomplished my goal even so," and held up a leather-bound book. Placing it on the table, he continued: "Although I did meet another wrangler, who arrived a few days before I did."

"And did he help you on your quest?" I asked, impatiently.

"Not the one I went to solve, and yet I think you will find him of interest. He rode away from the farm today, Tuesday, although he had arrived three days before I did, on Wednesday.

"How did he manage this, Watson?"

A RUBBISH TASK

The metropolitan police suffered a major fault in April of last year. We were called to a waste facility near Highgate, where a titanic task force was sifting through the rubbish in search of a series of important documents that had been accidentally disposed of by the service. It was a grim affair, though I felt thankful that we were visiting the facility in spring as opposed to the hot, sticky, stench-ridden summer months.

These documents were vital for a case that Holmes and I were working on, and we had reached our wits' end. In order for the case to continue, the documents needed to be found, and, since we weren't busy with any other matter, it made sense to be on the scene in case they did manage to locate these metaphorical needles in the haystack.

To pass the time while we waited, Holmes would occasionally throw riddles at me to keep me on my toes. One time, as we gazed out over the towering mounds of rubbish before us, he asked, "What is thrown out whenever it's used, and yet recovered whenever it is no longer needed?"
What indeed?

A FERRY TRIP

A few summers ago, Holmes and I were taking a ferry across from West Kilbride to the Isle of Aaron in Scotland. We had received a letter from an islander claiming that their inn had become haunted in the most terrifying manner, and asking for our help in solving the mystery. I felt this was an excellent chance to debunk yet another of the many hundreds of supernatural claims that we had been called upon to adjudicate in just the past few years.

I read the note they had sent us aloud:

"First and foremost, I hope that this letter has found you well. For almost five years now, I have been tortured by strange noises and odd physical phenomena coming from the basement below the lobby of our inn. I fear it is the ghost of my late mother, but I cannot be sure. Perhaps she abhors her inability to obtain heavenly glory."

Holmes interrupted me, distracted as always by some irrelevant tangent. "First; almost; below; ghost; abhors; glory!" he proclaimed. "Six words I paid more attention to, lost in the rest of that noisy letter. But Watson, tell me what these words have in common?"

What is Holmes referring to?

THE LETTER JUMBLES FOUR

As I have mentioned, after we had exhausted the puzzles in *The Strand Magazine*, Holmes and I would turn to our brainteasers.

One we particularly liked was the letter jumble game. For this, one of us would speak a word to the other, along with a number. The other party would then have five minutes to find that given number of jumbles of the letters of the other words.

Let me repeat my example, to clarify matters somewhat. Say that the word was SKATE and the number was three, then the jumbles would be STAKE, STEAK, and TAKES. All use the same letters, but in a different order, while still being legitimate words.

Here is another of our puzzles:

PADRES. Five

Can you find all the jumbles?

THE GREEK PATH

In a daring mission to intercept a group of high-earning spice smugglers, Holmes and I journeyed to Cyprus, stopping off in Athens along the way. There, we promenaded around the ancient ruins and sampled delicious Mediterranean cuisine. It was such an enjoyable weekend that I came away with a strong urge to move out there permanently. But then again, I don't think I could face the effort of learning another language. Not again.

"Such a rich history," I said to Holmes, "richer than even London herself."

He grunted.

"It is interesting to think how far we have come in the last century. I might even say that the last hundred years have made us more advanced than the thousand years before it!" I pontificated.

Holmes snorted at this, saying "Indeed, Watson? You make me think of a man who lived in 1630, who had no gas lights, or locomotives to travel on. Imagine, in such a year he turned forty years of age, much like us today.

"But then, imagine this: in 1640 he was not fifty, as we would now expect, but he was merely thirty years of age.

"Can you explain this more modern change in ageing, Watson?"

MRS HUDSON'S AGE

As all right-minded people know, it is highly impertinent to ask a woman about her age. And should she ever ask you to guess, you should always say "as bright and youthful as that of twenty and one." It cannot fail.

If you are Sherlock Holmes, on the other hand, you can discard all semblance of manners simply because that is who you are. So, when Mrs Hudson waltzed into the living room one day, I was not surprised to hear him speak bluntly to her from across the room, "Mrs Hudson, how old are you today?"

Now, she is such a graceful lady that she did not hesitate to give us an answer, and did it in the most charming of ways. "On my last birthday I turned seventy-three," she said.

"And you look fifty-two fewer!" I cried, earning myself a steely gaze from Holmes.

She ignored my efforts to compliment her, and continued, "and on my next birthday, I shall be turning seventy-five!"

At this, Holmes quickly rose to his feet and apologized to Mrs Hudson for his rudeness.

Why did he choose that moment to remember his manners?

THE TRANSATLANTIC TRIP

Holmes once went for some months to North America, and not long after his return began a never-ending barrage of reports on his adventures, interspersed with anecdotes and the occasional riddle. Indeed, it seemed Holmes had an endless supply of the latter. To be fair to the man, however, even the dullest of his stories usually turned out to be interesting.

One thing that particularly amazed him was the astounding transcontinental railroad that had opened a few decades prior to the trip.

"Recall, Watson, that when you travel up to Edinburgh by rail the journey seems to last for days; but the rail journey I speak of, which stretches from New York to San Francisco, truly does. Of course, my outward trip towards the Rockies and then beyond, to the west coast itself, was broken up by various investigatory visits. But my journey home, from west to east, was entirely uninterrupted. Even so, it took three and a half days."

"How on earth did you occupy yourself for such a time?" I asked. "I hope there were at least a few murderers on the train?" I then quickly added, "Retired ones, of course."

"I watched the country roll past, with its vast array of scenery to observe. And I also counted the number of trains I saw passing in the opposite direction."

"Were there many?" I asked.

"Well, you can work it out for yourself, Watson. Trains departed from

San Francisco and New York at exactly the same time every twelve hours. Given that it took three and a half days to reach New York from San Francisco, and assuming that all the trains were moving at exactly the same speed without stopping (a bit of an approximation, but it will suffice for this question), then how many locomotives were at some point level with me on the opposing tracks?"

A FRAGILE SITUATION

A nasty murder led Holmes to fly across London like a bee to a wild flower garden. The victim, Walter Norris, was an avid crystal-glass collector, and had been stabbed through the heart with a broken shard. His home was a marvel to behold, if one ignored the body, and reminded me of a description I had once heard of an ice cave. Hundreds of glass ornaments adorned the walls, tables, and even the floor. As a result, and so as to not disturb the crime scene, we were required to move very carefully throughout the home.

"So much fragile glass," I said. "I could not live in a home such as this, but I feel glad to have paid it a visit."

"And yet sometimes you treasure something remarkably fragile of your own; so fragile indeed that you could break it just by saying its name," Holmes responded.

What was he referring to?

THE LINKS
IN THE STRAND FOUR

On those occasions when our preferred word puzzle, the pyramid, was not included in an issue of *The Strand Magazine*, we would turn to its other regular puzzle, Link Words.

This puzzle worked via the need to find a so-called link word between two otherwise disconnected words. This link word could be added to the end of one, and the start of another, to form two entirely new further words.

Let me repeat the example I have given you previously. Say that you are given END and SHOT. You could then link them with the word EAR. How so, you may ask? Well, you would be forming ENDEAR, and EARSHOT, which are both words in our English dictionary.

Now here are three more for you to try yourself, all abiding by the same rules:

MINCE _ _ _ _ BALL

TAR _ _ _ RING

SIX _ _ _ _ AGE

What are the link words?

The "TANKS." By Col. E. D. SWINTON. FIRST AUTHORITATIVE ACCOUNT.

SOUTHAMPTON
STREET

THE STRAND MAGAZINE

SHERLOCK HOLMES
Outwits
A GERMAN SPY

You can send this Magazine Post Free to the Troops.
See Page 320.

Nº 321
VOL 54

8 d.
net.

Published monthly by GEORGE NEWNES, Ltd., 8 to 11, Southampton Street, Strand, London, England.

THE CIRCUS PINOCCHIO

Every so often, a circus visits London. Holmes would often remind me that, while there are many spectacles to behold, such popular entertainment has a tendency to attract the criminal element. As a result, he often insists that we attend because, in his eyes, it is a "breeding ground for crime, and who knows what he might find?" I have always suspected this to be a thinly veiled excuse for his own enjoyment of the event, but I am happy to go along.

One time we were at an exhibit of biological rarities, and came upon a man with the longest nose I had ever seen. We had no more than a glimpse of the man before we were shepherded, along with the rest of the crowd, into the next show tent; but for a brief moment I thought his nose must have been twelve inches or more. When I mentioned this to Holmes, however, he laughed and said that "No nose can ever be twelve inches long."

I observed from the expression on his face that he thought he was being extremely clever, but I knew at once what he meant. What?

A LUGGAGE COMPLICATION

We were awaiting the arrival of a large sea vessel in Portsmouth, with plans to search the suitcases of several suspects whom we believed to be aboard. It was a luxury liner that had unveiled a new system of delivering its upper-class passengers' luggage directly to their homes, to rid them of the stresses of directing their servants to deliver their belongings home after the journey.

Holmes and I gathered up the suitcases of five different, unrelated suspects in a quiet sorting room at the dockyard. Our search unfortunately yielded no further information, much to our disappointment. In our haste to operate quickly, however, I accidentally mixed up the destination addresses for the luggage.

I was unsure about whose bag was whose, so in the end I decided to randomly assign them their addresses and hope for the best. As we left, I remarked, "If we sent only one suitcase to an incorrect address, I would certainly call that a victory!"

"Then that is a victory you shall certainly not have, Watson."

Why not?

AT THE OPERA

Holmes makes a point of attending various cultural events in order (he claims) that "he can understand all levels of society." As a result, we secured tickets for an operatic performance in London's West End. It was a small space with only fifty seats, making the performance feel all the more exclusive. Holmes and I joined the back of the line of waiting ticketholders, somewhat late, but it seemed that they had not opened the doors yet. Holmes counted the heads ahead of us and commented that it would be a full house.

When the doors did finally open, there was still no movement. Through the commotion, I heard that the gentleman at the very front of the line had forgotten his seat number, and so was asked to take a seat at random. After this, the rest of us would enter to take our assigned seat, but if our seat was taken we would need to pick a different one, also at random. I realized, with a sinking feeling, that since I would be the last to enter, I would surely have almost no chance of being given my assigned seat.

Was I right? What is the probability that my ticketed seat would still be free?

ANOTHER CIRCUS

If you recall, Holmes and I often attended the events at circuses. On one such visit, in one tent, I saw an extraordinary young woman contort herself into an impossible shape. How she did it, or whether she could eat within several days of such a feat, I could not imagine.

Immediately next to that memorable tent, Holmes and I were ushered into Madame Moonbeam's Mystery tent, where we were greeted by the eponymous fortune teller. The walls of her tent were decorated with all kinds of strange markings, including illustrations of the planets and stars, and seemingly random letters.

Madame Moonbeam bade us sit, and began running her fingers over a crystal ball, periodically flipping a tarot card onto the silk-covered table. Then, as a final card was placed, she gasped. "The Grim!" she cried.

I leaned over to Holmes, and mumbled in his direction, "It's always the Grim."

"I predict a grave future for you, Messieurs!" she whispered. The bad news delivered, Holmes and I were soon on our way.

"I hope you enjoyed that, Holmes. Clearly it is self-evident that no one can predict the future," I said.

"On the contrary, Watson, predicting the future is entirely possible," said Holmes. "Even I could do it, should I wish to do so."

How can this be true?

TAVERN TRICKS

Holmes was in an unusually jovial mood one evening, which culminated in some drinks at a local hostelry.

"Forget the case, Watson! Let me show you something else that might pique your interest," Holmes said to me during a third round of drinks, as he pulled out his coin purse. "For now, I would like you to think of me as something of a prestidigitator."

"A simple trickster, or a gentleman con?" I queried.

"Hush now," he said, "and watch."

He emptied his purse onto the table, and counted what was there. "So, we have ten coins. But I now ask you, Watson, to mix up these coins, turning them over until a number of your choices show heads, while the rest show tails. But wait. First, I shall close my eyes and look away."

I eventually indicated that I was ready.

"Excellent, Watson. I shall still not look, but pray now tell me how many coins show heads."

I told him.

"And now, without seeing or feeling the coins, I will arrange them into two piles. And, I guarantee, each will have the exact same number of heads as the other!"

Keeping one hand over his eyes, Holmes then separated the coins into two groups. There was some flipping involved, but by the end he truly had two groups with the same number of heads.

How did he do it? It may help to try this out for yourself.

THE STRAND
PYRAMID FIVE

Here is a fifth of that particular puzzle from *The Strand Magazine* which both Holmes and I enjoyed.

As a reminder, the puzzle was built from words. The only confusion, however, was that the words themselves were not given, but rather clues. It was up to the reader to discover the words.

To assist in this task, a particular property was noted. Each clue was solved using the same set of letters as the word before, but with the addition of one further letter. The letters could, however, then be jumbled as you pleased. It might also be worth stating that the first clue was always solved by a three-letter word, and that the pyramid was built (somewhat improbably) from the top downwards.

Here is that fifth pyramid puzzle:

1. Female deer
2. Encryption method
3. Furnishings in general
4. Gained points in a game
5. Makes a note of an event, perhaps
6. Rusts

Can you solve it?

MOUSE MATHEMATICS

As I turned to walk down 221B Baker Street during my morning walk, I saw Holmes standing outside the house, smoking his pipe, and eyeing up a plank of wood that was held up between two A-frames.

"Good morning, Holmes!" I said. "What finds you out on the street this morning?"

"Morning, Watson. I have discovered a number of mouse holes around the flat," he replied.

"Oh, how dreadful!" I said.

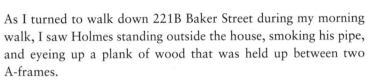

"Quite the opposite, in fact. For I have been encouraging their arrival and studying how they behave. I find that certain instincts, and responses to danger, map remarkably well to the human psyche," he insisted.

"I see. Don't they have laboratories for that?"

"Well, they aren't performing my experiments, are they? In any case, unfortunately Mrs Hudson has requested that I board up the holes because they have been getting into her cupboards."

Holmes held up a long wood saw, and pointed it in my general direction.

"But answer me this. If I cut this plank in two, at some random point along its length, then how long would I expect the smaller part to be?

Lestrade called Holmes and myself into the station one day, after he had received a letter that seemingly required desperate and immediate attention. Several months prior to this meeting, a wealthy magnate from Wandsworth had disappeared under suspicious circumstances. An associate of hers, Mr Everett Montgomery, had then forwarded the letter to Lestrade for further analysis, who had then called us in to do the same. The note read:

> *Dearest Everett,*
>
> *You will be wondering where your colleague is being held. She is in no immediate danger, but should you attempt to locate her, we will need to take additional measures to relocate her into harm's way.*
>
> *I shall not reveal her location, save to say that the country in which she now resides has precisely four letters in its name and is far out of the reach of Europe.*
>
> *Yours,*
> *Her kidnapper*

"So where has she gone?" I asked, perhaps rather simply.
"Well, I can think of a number of four-letter countries," said Holmes.
How many four-letter countries, all outside Europe, can you think of?

A MYSTERY WEAPON

In the morgue at St. Bartholomew's lay a body, but the exact details of its owner's unfortunate demise were a mystery to the staff there.

Holmes and I arrived to look further into the matter, and I am sorry to say that the combination of unusual stab markings told a rather unpleasant story.

Holmes leaned over the body and looked at it intently, running his finger along the wounds. "Interesting," he said, "though now I see it, it does not seem such an unusual death. Yes, perhaps at first, but once you know what the murder weapon is, or rather what the weapons are, it seems obvious."

"Indeed, Holmes?" I asked.

"Yes. Consider, Watson, what you would buy to eat and yet never actually eat?" said Holmes.

I realized this was an oblique hint. What were the murder weapons?

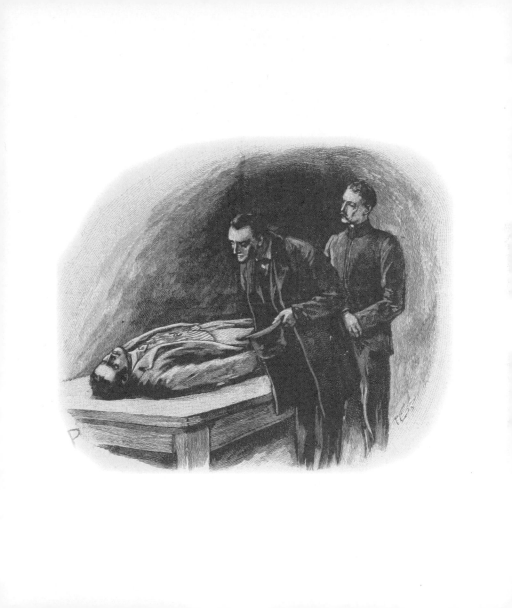

THE WORLD'S FAIR

I am fortunate to have attended the World's Fair in Paris. It was a dazzling production. I had gone there for personal interest, keen to observe the grand event with my own eyes, having read the many newspaper reports.

While there, an event transpired that soon shifted my purpose. While speaking to a stand keeper at the Argentine pavilion, I learned of a phrase that I feel is particularly relevant here: el mundo es pañuelo. It is a saying that you might utter when unexpectedly bumping into a friend or acquaintance in a place far from their usual dwelling.

So, you can imagine my surprise when I ran across a certain Sherlock Holmes outside of the grand Eiffel Tower. "El mundo es pañuelo!" I said, confidently. "Dash it all, Holmes, what on earth are you doing in Paris? You swore to me that you had no interest in attending!"

At my moment of arrival, Holmes was gazing up at the tower through a small pair of binoculars, which I quickly recognized as being my own. "Oh, greetings to you, Watson! I thought you might be around somewhere! Actually I arrived just a few hours ago. A frivolous affair, I assure you. We must journey up to the top of this structure if you are not too deterred by its height!" he said, gesturing to the Tower.

Holmes and I entered into the lift in one of the legs of the Eiffel Tower. It was an incredible contraption. On one side of the lift I saw the ornate panel of buttons for each floor. At the bottom of the panel was a button that read 0, denoting the ground level, and these buttons continued up to the top of the panel, finishing at the number 5 at around eye level to indicate a higher level of the tower

On our way up, Holmes told me about a mild mystery that he had encountered following a conversation with one of the Tower's guards. A child of one of the guards, aged only six or seven, would sneak into the elevator when it was closed in order to journey up the leg.

"But here's the thing. The boy never took the elevator all the way. Consistently, he would stop a level short and then walk the rest of the way up," Holmes explained.

"And why do you think that was, Watson?"

THE GEARED DOOR

A pursuit of Moriarty sent Holmes and myself down into one of London's many subterranean tunnels.

The air was thick and hot, and rats scurried past us, thankfully keen to be anywhere other than where we were. When we finally reached the end of the tunnel, we were greeted by an impressive doorway. There were a number of levers on the ground, and next to them were two large circular gears, both of the same size, stacked on top of one another.

A closer look showed that the bottom gear was held in place and would not move, but the upper gear could rotate on a circular track around the outside of it. Together they formed part of a door mechanism, which worked in a way I could not immediately fathom.

Holmes, of course, took the opportunity for a riddle:

"If you rotate the upper gear all the way around the lower one, and back to where it began, then how many revolutions would that upper gear have made?"

A certain case called for Holmes and myself to meet with an astronomer of the Royal Observatory in Greenwich, one Dr Boulton. You may also recall that, during a trip to the fair with Holmes, we had encountered an astrologist by the name of Madame Moonbeam, who we were now investigating as an accomplice and/or key witness to a serious crime.

While waiting near the astronomer's office, my gaze strayed onto a wall chart. There, I saw lettering that matched letters I had previously seen on the walls of the fortune-teller's tent. A crack in the case, or so I thought! The letters were:

"Y S H S R N S E".

I nudged Holmes and gestured to the chart, saying, "I think they might be involved with each other, Holmes!" But Holmes merely laughed.

"Is something the matter?" Boulton asked, entering the room.

"No, in fact Watson here was just admiring the artistry of your wall chart," he said to Boulton. Moments later, he leaned towards me and muttered, "I admire your deduction, Watson, but I assure you that it is perfectly reasonable for both parties to have that set of letters lying around."

What did the letters mean?

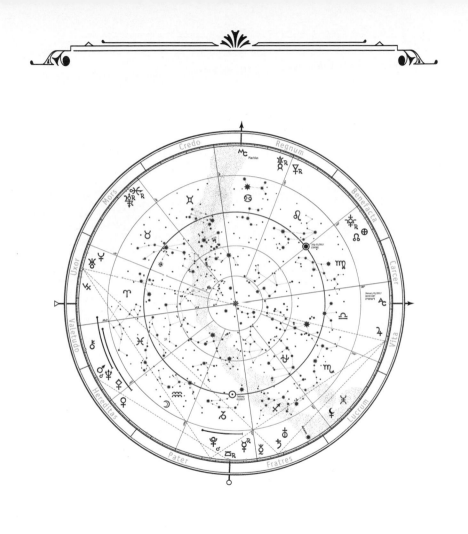

THE
ISLAND ESCAPE

"Watson, a thought experiment for you," said Holmes one day.

He continued, "I want you to use your imagination and picture yourself on a desert island. A remote one, where there is no chance of anyone coming to rescue you."

"And I have to work out how to escape?" I guessed.

"Yes. But you have no tools or belongings of any sort, no transport, and the island is too far from land to swim away from.

"Now, what is the quickest way to escape?"

What is it?

BEHIND THE
GEARED DOOR

I have already related how Holmes and I, in pursuit of Moriarty, had found an underground door with a complex geared mechanism. After some effort we opened the door successfully, and found ourselves in a large cavern. A

strange ticking sound filled the air.

A man stood near to three further doors at the far side of the cavern. We approached with caution, our lamp held high. Through the murky air, it suddenly became apparent that the cavern was lined with dynamite; perhaps more than I had ever seen in one single place. The ticking became louder, and I was shocked to see wires running to batches of dynamite.

The man, who was strangely well-dressed for an underground dweller, laughed menacingly when

he saw us. "Ah, there you are. We have been expecting you!" he cried. "But Moriarty will be disappointed. He thought you would find this place much more quickly."

"Who are you? What is this place?" I asked.

The man replied, "I am afraid there is no more time for pleasantries, for we stand in the caverns beneath Buckingham Palace, and there are only moments left to spare before this dynamite explodes.

"But Mr Moriarty enjoys a game, and he will offer you a chance to save the Palace. And yourselves, I might add.

"Before you lie three doors. Behind one, you will be granted the means to stop the explosion. Behind the others... nothing. Pick the right door and live. Pick the wrong door and... well, you will go down in history, along with the palace above."

"Stop this nonsense, man. What is it that you want?" I shouted.

He ignored me, seemingly oblivious. "Pick a door", he said, "and then I shall pick a door too. I know where the bomb timer is, so I guarantee you that I will open a door that does not conceal it. But, to be even fairer, I will then give you the chance to change your choice of door, should you wish to."

"I know what we should do," Holmes reassured me, quietly. "But it may be best if you leave, Watson."

"I will not leave your side, Holmes," I replied.

When he is given the chance, should Holmes stay with the door he chooses from the start, or swap it for the other door? Which gives him the best chance of surviving?

THE LINKS
IN *THE STRAND* FIVE

On those occasions when our preferred word puzzle, the pyramid, was not included in an issue of *The Strand Magazine*, we would turn to its other regular puzzle, Link Words.

This puzzle worked via the need to find a so-called link word between two otherwise disconnected words. This link word could be added to the end of one, and the start of another, to form two entirely new further words.

Let me repeat the example I have given you previously. Say that you are given END and SHOT. You could then link them with the word EAR. How so, you may ask? Well, you would be forming ENDEAR, and EARSHOT, which are both words in our English dictionary.

Now here are three more for you to try yourself, all abiding by the same rules:

BREAK _ _ _ _ _ PROOF

CROSS _ _ _ LED

SWIM _ _ _ _ CASE

What are the link words?

THE PALACE GARDENS

"You never cease to amaze me," I said to Holmes, as we climbed out of a storm drain and into the Buckingham Palace gardens. "How did you know that the bomb timer was behind the other door?"

"Truth be told, Watson, I didn't know," he replied. I was startled. The great Sherlock Holmes had to guess?

"Dash it all, Holmes!" I stammered, while trying to remain quiet enough not to alert the palace guards.

"It was a simple matter of chance. But I had no other choice, lest the palace be blown to smithereens by the hand of the ticking timer," he said.

We made our way quietly to the side of the garden, and then began to search around the edge for an exit.

After a minute or two of unsuccessful searching, Holmes said that it would help me to pass the time if I could tell him, "What is forever running around this garden, and yet will never move at all?"

Apparently it was riddle time again. What was his expected answer?

The Tomb Aiders

In the tombs of an ancient city whose name I am forbidden to disclose, Holmes and I once found ourselves in search of clues. We came upon a certain room, in which nine shadowy artefacts were arranged, lit by a thin beam of light. They were arranged like this:

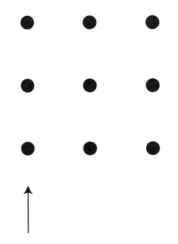

The arrow shows where the beam of light was shining in, and it cast its light on three of the items.

For reasons too intricate to disclose, we needed to reflect that beam of light so that not just three but rather all nine objects were lit. We had with us three mirrors, that we could place where we wished. How could we place them in order to reflect the light as required?

To solve this conundrum, it may help to imagine the beams of light as four straight lines that form a single path. How can you draw those lines to that they visit all nine points?

THE ALCHEMIST'S LAMENT

I had recently come across a puzzle in a journal and decided to test it on Holmes. One day, therefore, I found myself asking him, "Which is heavier, Holmes: a pound of lead or a pound of feathers?"

He replied immediately, saying "They are the same weight, Watson," before continuing, "Did you think that would catch me out? It is a riddle that confuses some, I grant you, since it uses misdirection to hide the readily given information.

"But we can make it more interesting. Let us take it a step further.

"Say I have a set of weighing scales, and I submerge those scales entirely in water. Now, to continue, I must change the materials you have given here, as feathers are not dense enough to sink in water. So, instead, say I wish to weigh a pound of gold against a pound of lead.

"Now, when I weigh these two metals underwater, which will show as heavier on the scales?"

What was the correct answer?

THE REVERSIBLE WORDS

Holmes and I would occasionally challenge each other with small quizzes.

On one occasion, I came across some interesting words and challenged him to find words that could describe both of the things I mentioned, on reflection. By this, I meant that when the letters were read in their traditional ordering, one meaning would arise; but when reversed, the other meaning would be indicated.

As an example, if I said "the core of the matter; and a bread roll," then the answer would be NUB / BUN.

Here are three I particularly liked:
Uses scissors; turns around
Suffered from angst; puddings
One who ransacks; repurpose a device
Can you solve them?

VOLTAIRE'S TEASER

Lounging on the couch while reading a volume of Voltaire's philosophical writings, Holmes suddenly let out a loud "ha!", which I feel sure was at least in part simply to gain my attention. Initially I ignored him but, when he began to chuckle with apparent purpose, I had no choice but to offer him my ears.

"Reading Voltaire again, I see. Come then, share with me some of your discoveries," I said.

"The man has such a way with words," Holmes remarked. "But, truth be told, the primary reason for voicing my amusement was because I wanted to steal your attention for a moment. Let me read you this passage:

"What of all things in the world is the longest, the shortest, the swiftest, the slowest, the most divisible and most extended, most regretted, most neglected, without which nothing can be done, and with which many can do nothing, which destroys all that is little and ennobles all that is great?"

I must admit that receiving a riddle from one of the philosophical greats felt a great deal more noble than the sorts of huckster riddles that Holmes continually thrust upon me. So, with more pleasure than normal, I thought on this further.

What did Voltaire refer to?

A STUDY IN PINK

Holmes and I paid a return visit to renowned French mathematician Marie Lecloud to offer our thanks. She had helped us in a case that involved a closed water system, as I am sure you will remember, especially given that it was front-page news only weeks ago.

On a large chalkboard, Marie seemed to be working on an odd sequence of figures, which I imagined to be an advanced equation that even Holmes would not be able to understand.

"My humblest of welcomes to you both. Knowledge is but an unlimited chalice from which we pour unto others," she pronounced.

"Rehearse that one, did you?" Holmes asked, rather brutally.

"Off the cuff," she replied, adding, "Sherlock, perhaps you should try to add a dash more poetry to your vocabulary, instead of leaving it to those who do not speak the language, such as moi."

"Language and flair are two diffident bedfellows, Madame. They can coexist without needing to procreate such florid sentences as your own. But you have been busy I see," he said, gesturing to the chalkboard.

"Indeed! In fact, I rather hoped you might help me solve this one," she said. "It could do with the touch of a man such as you."

I looked at the puzzling set of characters, which read:

$$\omega \eth\!\int\!f \quad \mu^p \quad \mu^{5}\!\varphi \quad \lceil\alpha\rceil\!\forall\!f \quad \mathcal{W}\!\mathcal{A} \quad q^{6}\!\eth\!\imath$$

"Don't keep the lady waiting!" I said to Holmes, cheerfully. "Well what does it say?"

Holmes had fallen unusually quiet. What did the message say?

THE CASINO JOB

I would venture a guess that, since our investigatory antics have become public knowledge, the victims and witnesses we interview have made an effort to become rather more cryptic. Perhaps they fear that Holmes can see right through

them, or perhaps the rationale is one of public exposure. If I report on a case and a witness decides to make their statement more of a talking point, they will surely receive more recognition from my readers than if they had given the most tedious of answers.

In a recent case we found ourselves at a casino from which a certain thief had stolen a great amount from their vault. What was so baffling in this case was that the owner of the casino, and our client for the case, told us about the crime in the most cryptic of manners. In fact, I half suspected it was all a publicity stunt.

Nonetheless, we listened keenly. It was suggested that we seek out and question three of the man's colleagues, but were not given their names. The owner claimed that, upon solving his clue, their identities would become obvious to us. I practically heard Holmes' eyes roll in their sockets, but we allowed him to continue and share such a hint.

The owner began, "The man and his colleagues will frequently sit down in the casino and play all night, and let it be clear that they play for money. Or if they do play for fun, I have never seen them do so, and

certainly not in my casino. But here is what will allow you to identify them, for they have the unique characteristic that they always leave the casino having gained money. No one ever loses, and yet I allow them to return every night."

Holmes snorted.

The owner continued, "Telling tales about my guests and my staff is bad for business. I'm sure you understand. So this is all I can say. The rest you will need to deduce for yourselves."

Who were the people we should question?

THE LETTER JUMBLES FIVE

As I have mentioned, after we had exhausted the puzzles in *The Strand Magazine*, Holmes and I would turn to our brainteasers.

One we particularly liked was the letter jumble game. For this, one of us would speak a word to the other, along with a number. The other party would then have five minutes to find that given number of jumbles of the letters of the other words.

Let me repeat my example, to clarify matters somewhat. Say that the word was SKATE and the number was three, then the jumbles would be STAKE, STEAK, and TAKES. All use the same letters, but in a different order, while still being legitimate words.

Here is another of our puzzles:

SPRIEST. Three

Can you find all the jumbles?

THE CASINO RIDDLE

Shortly after we left the casino, having passed through the restaurant on our way to a side exit, Holmes set me a riddle:

"Watson, answer me this. In that building we just left, what is put on the tables and then cut but never consumed?"

I felt that it was likely to be some kind of foodstuff, but I must admit I struggled to find an answer. What did Holmes intend?

Sherlock Holmes has a reputation around this country, and such fame attracts a large number of fanatics. Indeed, I will often sift through the incoming mail to find the letters that appear important, and then save the rest for those special evenings in which we indulge ourselves in strangers' compliments and questions.

In among these letters we sometimes find riddles. One that I recently enjoyed read as follows:

Wherever I go, my brother's just been.

He is seen but not heard; I am heard but not seen.

Now say who we are; from the above you can glean.

Of course, Holmes knew the answer immediately. What was it?

THE FLOWERY LANGUAGE

I once entered 221B to discover Holmes tending to an absurd number of plants. Having decided that he had insufficient knowledge on the activities of plant propagators and breeders, he had taken it upon himself to rectify this with a range of plants all held within one small room.

"Indeed, Watson," he began, after explaining just why the plants were so important, "It turns out that making sure they feed and drink at the right times, and in the right amounts, is much more important than you might suspect.

"That said, can you tell me what it is that needs to be fed to stay alive, but dies if given a drink?"

"I think you could do with eating more and drinking less, Holmes," I replied, suspecting wine on an empty stomach as the original cause of this strange thinking.

What was the answer to his riddle?

THE STRAND PYRAMID SIX

We continued to avidly read *The Strand Magazine* for its word pyramid puzzle.

As a reminder, the puzzle was built from words. However, the words themselves were not given, but rather clues. It was up to the us to discover the words.

Each clue was solved using the same set of letters as the word before, but with the addition of one further letter. The letters could, however, then be jumbled as you pleased. It might also be worth stating that the first clue was always solved by a three-letter word, and that the pyramid was built (somewhat improbably) from the top downward.

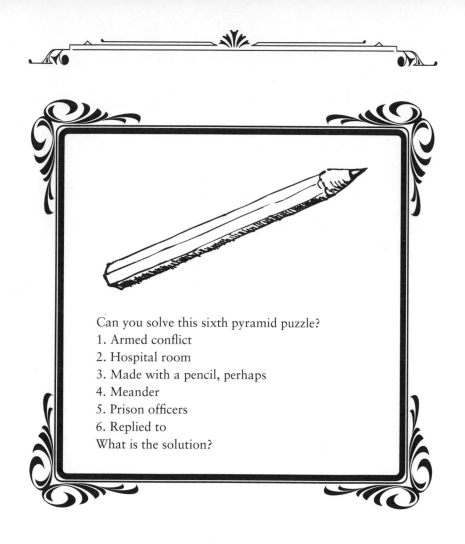

Can you solve this sixth pyramid puzzle?
1. Armed conflict
2. Hospital room
3. Made with a pencil, perhaps
4. Meander
5. Prison officers
6. Replied to
What is the solution?

THE IDENTICAL TAGS

One day, I accompanied Holmes and Inspector Lestrade to the morgue at St. Bartholomew's to work on a case.

An underground tunnel had collapsed, killing two workers at the same time, and the bodies had been tagged in a way that had confused Lestrade. In particular, he was concerned by the seemingly inconsistent way in which the bodies had been identified, since he had expected them to have matching tags.

One body had a label stating 1100 + 20, while the other read 1200 – 40.

Holmes took a look at them, then announced, "Lestrade, they're identical."

And sure enough, the labels were indeed intended to mean the same thing. What had Holmes realized?

On those occasions when our preferred word puzzle, the pyramid, was not included in an issue of *The Strand Magazine*, we would turn to its other regular linking-words puzzle.

This puzzle worked via the need to find a so-called link word between two otherwise disconnected words. This link word could be added to the end of one, and the start of another, to form two entirely new further words.

Let me repeat the example I have given you previously. Say that you are given END and SHOT. You could then link them with the word EAR. How so, you may ask? Well, you would be forming ENDEAR, and EARSHOT, which are both words in our English dictionary.

Now here are three more for you to try yourself, all abiding by the same rules:

FOOTS _ _ _ _ BAR

HEAD _ _ _ _ _ _ HOLD

PANT _ _ _ RINGS

What are the link words?

ALL MIXED UP

We were on the tail of the Baskerville Boys, a juvenile gang that felt themselves the height of cleverness by naming themselves after one of Holmes' most publicized cases.

They seemed to think that it was their duty to society (and perhaps my literary musings) to leave clues to their crimes littering the scenes of each of their robberies.

On one particular case I came across the following message, left behind on a park bench. I immediately identified that it was likely to be an anagram, but what did it say?

WASN'T TUTORS

Holmes identified it as two words, which I felt was obvious until he explained that the correct letters were not in the correct words, but that three letters from each would need to swap from one side to the other before the anagrams were solved.

What did the message say? As a clue, it made Holmes laugh.

THE LETTER JUMBLES SIX

As I have mentioned, after we had exhausted the puzzles in *The Strand Magazine*, Holmes and I would turn to our brainteasers.

One we particularly liked was the letter jumble game. For this, one of us would speak a word to the other, along with a number. The other party would then have five minutes to find that given number of jumbles of the letters of the other words.

"'NOTHING COULD BE BETTER,' SAID HOLMES."

Let me repeat my example, to clarify matters somewhat. Say that the word was SKATE and the number was three, then the jumbles would be STAKE, STEAK, and TAKES. All use the same letters, but in a different order, while still being legitimate words.

Here is another of our puzzles:

TRAINERS. Three

Can you find all the jumbles?

FURTHER REVERSIBLE WORDS

Holmes and I occasionally challenged each other with small quizzes, and some of these quizzes proved successful enough that we would revisit the idea at a later date.

Previously, I had come across some interesting words and challenged Holmes to find words that could describe both of the things I mentioned, on reflection. By this, I meant that when the letters were read in their traditional ordering, one meaning would arise; but when reversed, the other meaning would be indicated. As an example, if I had said "the core of the matter; and a bread roll," then the answer would be NUB / BUN.

Holmes later repaid the complement with three similar puzzles of his own. Here they are:

Prepares oneself; precipitates icily
Extremely disliked; come through
Prepares a potato, perhaps; slumber

Can you solve them?

THE HOUNDS OF THE BASKERVILLES

The Baskerville Boys were always very proud of their cleverness, and on one occasion they left a large litter of puppies in a central London highway, accompanied by a note that proclaimed them to be the Hounds of the Baskervilles. Even Holmes admitted a wry smile to his face when he heard of this.

Three of the puppies were Dalmatians, and I amused myself by counting the number of spots on them. I observed the following:

The first puppy had 7 fewer spots than the second, and 12 fewer than the third.

The first and third puppy, when considered together, had 42 spots.

How many spots did each puppy have?

THE TITLE DEED

"Would you sign this for me, please?" Holmes said one day, handing over a contract that he had already signed himself.

"And what is this?" I asked, sensibly.

"A deed. I am buying a small island in Scotland, and I need a witness to my signing."

"How small?"

Holmes paused, then replied, "Around half a hectare. But I require that you ask no more."

At this, I began flicking through the document to ensure I was not signing up for some ghoulish medical experiment. I did not entirely put it past the man.

Holmes, waiting for me to sign, began thoughtfully spinning the globe in the corner of the room. Then, seemingly tiring of waiting, he could not help but to ask me a riddle. "Watson! While you read that contract, tell me this: What is it that is always stuck in a single

place, and yet so often travels around the world?"

"I implore that you only ask me to do one thing at a time, Holmes," I replied, and then absentmindedly signed while trying to solve the darn riddle.

What was the answer?

SOLUTIONS

THE WARRIOR WOMEN 10
Holmes observed that I was describing the pieces in a game of chess.

AN ORDERED SEQUENCE 12
E. The sequence is the initial letters of the ordinal numbers in increasing order: first, second, third, etc.

A HAT-TRICK 13
I hung my hat on the barrel of my gun, so it was impossible to miss.

***THE STRAND* PYRAMID ONE** 15
SEE; EASE; EAVES; LEAVES; SEVERAL; CLEAVERS.

SOCIETY RIDDLES 16
History.

THE GAP YEAR 19
We spoke to the boy on January 1st. On December 30th just gone, he had been 13, then had his 14th birthday on the next day, December 31st. He is therefore turning 15 on the last day of this year, so will turn 16 on the last day of next year.

A STRANGE CASE 20
1678. Other, higher, combinations are 2389, 2569, 3478 and 4567.

A FAIR AFFAIR 22
The man was a parachutist, and the unopened package was his parachute that had failed to open.

LOOKING APART 25
They were facing each other the entire time. In such a situation, they would indeed be facing in opposite directions.

SOLUTIONS

A disease; perhaps she was thinking of the disease that was claiming her life.

A tongue, which certainly can taste very well but cannot smell at all.

She killed her sister in the hopes that the man of her dreams would be at the second family funeral, too. Her obsession had driven her mad.

O. They are the initials of the elements of the periodic table in increasing atomic weight, starting at hydrogen and working upward.

The maid. There is no post on Sundays, so she must have lied in her alibi.

He was a priest.

A reflection.

All of the letters need to be shifted 5 letters down the alphabet to read.
   The message says: COME TO ST PANCRAS TRAIN STATION AT THREE IN THE AFTERNOON THIS FRIDAY.

SOLUTIONS

SISTERLY LOVE

Because he would be dead. If his wife is a widow, he himself is dead, and he could therefore neither physically nor legally marry his wife's sister.

THE BEAR NECESSITIES

A polar bear. The only place on earth where all sides are facing south would be at the north pole, which would make the bear a polar bear. (I doubt Holmes ventured that far; I rather think he made this up to test me).

CHILDISH NAMES

The child's name is Elizabeth. Mrs Hudson said that Elizabeth's mother had four children, so Elizabeth must be the fourth child.

TWO LORDS AND TWO LADIES

They are both simultaneously stepfather and stepson to one another.

A TRAY GLASS

I had hiccups. The barman scared the hiccups out of me, and thus there was no need for the glass of water.

THE IMPOSSIBLE LINE

Fold the paper in a concertina shape so that the rightmost X falls in line with the other two, and then connect the three together with a normal straight line.

GONE TO THE DOGS

It will be in second place, not first place.

THE LINKS IN *THE STRAND*

STALL: FORESTALL and STALLIONS; LEDGE: KNOWLEDGE and LEDGERING; SAT: BABYSAT and SATIRE.

SOLUTIONS

THE RIDDLE THEORY 54
The word incorrectly is, naturally, always spelled like this: incorrectly.

SOCIAL SHAKES 56
No handshakes would take place, since anyone shorter than you would refuse to shake your hand, as you would be taller than them. (Just as he preferred it to be, commented Holmes).

LONDON ZOO ONE 57
A chair, or indeed a table.

THE LINKS IN *THE STRAND* TWO 58
BOOKS: LOGBOOKS and BOOKSHOP; LIME: SUBLIME and LIMELIGHT; RAIN: REFRAIN and RAINFALL.

A RUNNING HYPOTHESIS 59
No man raced because it was a woman's race. This was a most unusual occurrence, so it was hardly my first thought.

SHAKESPEARE'S WORK 60
Hamlet's uncle, Claudius, since he did murder most foul (fowl). Holmes thought this was hilarious, which said more about his mind than my own, I felt.

A REMARKABLE CALCULATION 63
"ELEVEN + TWO" and "TWELVE + ONE" are anagrams of each other.

THE RIDDLE SESSION ONE 64
The word "wholesome".

SOLUTIONS

RESIN, RINSE, RISEN, SIREN.

He fell off the bottom rung of a thirty-foot ladder, not the top. That is indeed "some" distance, just a rather short one.

Glass. Holmes had actually said greenhouse.

He is referring to a man who is a barber. He shaves several times a day, and yet it does not affect his own hair.

It was in a shoe.

He planned to sit inside the cube (which is more practical when building one as a piece of furniture), from whence he could turn his head to see every side.

A bee, since bear without ear is indeed just a b.

Benjamin is divorcing his current wife as a prelude to marrying Abigail instead.

They had once been part of a snowman that had since melted away.

SOLUTIONS

He opted to increase his salary by 9.5% every six months. Although the percentage rise is slightly less each year (19% once both are applied), receiving an increase earlier in the year always gives a greater total for the year.

For the 9.5% option, he will earn £50 and £54.75 in the first year for a total of £104.75; in the 20% option, he will earn £100 in the first year. In the second year, the 9.5% option will earn £59.95 and £65.65 for a total of £125.60, while the 20% option would earn £120 in the second year. So the second option is, relatively, worse than it was in the first year, and it only continues to get worse still over the following years.

A coin.

R. It is the first letters of the shades that make up a rainbow in reverse order, working from violet through to red.

The moon.

SAG; BAGS; GRABS; BARGES; BADGERS; ABRIDGES.

The height of the second shape is less than the original, despite its similar appearance. The total area lost by the height can now be found in the overhanging part of the rectangle.

SOLUTIONS

CANTER, NECTAR, TRANCE.

Each is equally pure. If one container loses x amount of its chemical, there must be an equal amount added to the other; therefore both have the same level of purity, albeit one for chemical A and the other for chemical B.

This may be easier to describe on a smaller scale. Imagine that I have two apples in one bowl and two oranges in another, and that I first put one of the apples in the orange bowl. I want to make sure that each bowl still has two pieces of fruit in it, so I now pick out a random fruit from the orange bowl and put it in the apple bowl. If I picked out an orange, the two bowls would contain the same amount of the opposite bowl's original fruit. If I pulled out an apple and put it back in its original bowl, both bowls would still contain the same amount of the opposite bowl's original fruit.

Envelope, which starts and ends with e, but often contains a single letter.

Your name.

ONES: OVERTONES and ONESELF; TIGHT: SKINTIGHT and TIGHTROPE; SING: DISCUSSING and SINGLED.

Start by turning both the five- and seven-minute sandglasses over together. Then, when the five-minute one is finished, turn it over and

SOLUTIONS

wait for the seven-minute one to reach zero. When it does, just turn the five-minute one back over, and two minutes of sand will run back through again, to give a timing of nine minutes overall.

The word noise. I cheated a little and wrote down my riddle phonetically, as Holmes might have heard it. The eye in the question is in fact the letter I, being removed to leave nose.

It is the initials of the French numbers from 1 to 10: un, deux, trois, quatre, cinq, six, sept, huit, neuf, and dix.

The minute and hour hands have been accidentally switched while it was being repaired.

Put a measured quantity of a marker substance into the system, and run the system so it is mixed and dispersed evenly throughout. Measure its concentration in various samples to find an estimate for the quantity of water relative to the quantity of marker, and then multiply the known quantity of water by its dilution. Luckily Holmes knew a chemist who knew just the substance to use.

The future.

You cannot overtake last place, because if you were behind them

SOLUTIONS

they would not be in last place! In a longer race, you might be able to overtake them by lapping them but, since this is a race of 200 yards, that can't be the case here.

ROD; ROAD; RADIO; ORDAIN; INROADS; DINOSAUR.

My voice.

The second man was arrested. You cannot fly the St George's Flag upside down.

Cover over the top half of the equation with a sheet of paper to reveal the true message:

I LOVE YOU

The black circles represent where the original counters were placed, and then moving from those four positions to new positions I created five lines of four coins as follows:

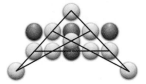

SOLUTIONS

If you cut horizontally through the middle of XI, the roman numerals for 11, discarding the bottom half, you get VI the roman numerals for 6.

The words are, in turn, startling, starling, staring, string, sting, sing, sin, in, and I.

He divided the land as follows:

An umbrella

A footstep.

The letter U.

You can get halfway into a forest, but after this you are then less than halfway from the other side.

PASTEL, PETALS, PLATES, PLEATS, STAPLE.

SOLUTIONS

The letter contains letters from an audio code alphabet. In order they are: Hotel echo Lima papa Mike echo, i.e. HELP ME.

He advised the brothers to ride each other's horse, meaning that whoever won the race would get the inheritance because the horse they owned would be the slower, losing horse.

Each pair of letters has been swapped around, so the message read: "BURGLARY TONIGHT. OXFORD STREET. MORIARTY".

R. They are the first books of the Old Testament, arranged in their customary order: Genesis, Exodus, Leviticus, Numbers, Deuteronomy, Joshua, Judges, Ruth. (Had Holmes been Jewish, he might also have answered S, for Samuel comes next in the Torah).

The assistant. Periodic Table elements 5, 8, and 39 are Boron, Oxygen, and Yttrium, whose chemical symbols are B, O, and Y. So the test tubes spelled out BOY.

The match. Otherwise how would you light any of the others?

The window the man had jumped from was closed. If the man had committed suicide from the window, it was very unlikely he would have

SOLUTIONS

been able to close it neatly as he did so.

The first letters of each line, taken together, spell I LOVE YOU.

A mirror. She had simply caught sight of her reflection in the mirror over her dressing table. The noise was from the wind.

Happy Birthday

S. They are the initials of the taxonomic classification system of living things, starting at kingdom and then working through to species: kingdom, phylum, class, order, family, genus, species.

A candle and a box of matches. After lighting the candle, the light from it filled the entire room. (He might also have filled the room with a visible gas, although this would have been a more complex and perhaps pricey method.)

It was one volume of a multi-volume encyclopedia. This volume covered entries that started with the letters HOW up to entries starting with JOG.

Make haste Regent's Park centre. Only the capitalized words are to be read.

SOLUTIONS

The word anyone, since then you only have one left.

The doorman lets in those who answer with the number of letters in the word that he has told them.

James is telling the truth. If Abigail was telling the truth, then Gemma would have to be too. If Gemma was telling the truth, James would be telling the truth too. But if James is telling the truth, both Abigail and Gemma are lying.

A. DAY; YARD; READY; DEARLY; LAYERED; REPLAYED.

Seven. A worst-case scenario would result in two 1d, two 2d, and two 3d stamps being pulled out. In such a case, the seventh stamp is certain to deliver the third of a kind.

Since we knew where we had come from, all we needed to do was orientate the signpost so that the sign pointing to our previous location was behind us. Then we followed the sign to our destination as normal.

100%. Any three dots placed on a sphere will always appear on the same half, once you rotate the sphere appropriately.

A greeting.

SOLUTIONS

His horse was named Wednesday.

An anchor.

The letters in all six of these words are in alphabetical order.

DRAPES, PARSED, RASPED, SPARED, SPREAD.

The man was born in 1670 BCE.

He realized that it is Mrs Hudson's seventy-fourth birthday today.

Holmes passed fifteen trains. With two trains setting off per day, and
three and a half days' travel time, you would certainly expect to pass the
seven trains that set off as, or after, you do. But by the time you have set
off there are already three and a half days' worth of trains on the track
already. So, you pass the first of the seven trains that have already left as
you leave, and then pass the next six through until day two. On day two,
you begin passing trains that left after you did, which means another
seven trains. Then, as you are arriving, you pass another train just as it is
leaving the station.

Silence.

SOLUTIONS

MEAT: MINCEMEAT and MEATBALL; TAR: TARTAR and
TARRING; TEEN: SIXTEEN and TEENAGE.

If a nose were twelve inches long, it would be a foot. And, as Holmes
observed, "a foot is clearly not a nose." Which is rather lucky, given
some people's feet, I suppose.

It is impossible. If you had tagged four suitcases correctly, then the
final suitcase could not be incorrectly tagged. So the situation described
cannot arise.

Fifty-fifty.

Anyone can predict the future, but that does not mean their predictions
are accurate.

It is a simple mathematical trick that works with any number of coins.
The first thing to realize is that the groups of coins need not be equal
in number. One group will contain the number of coins you are told
have been flipped to show heads, the second group will contain all the
remaining coins. Next flip all coins in this first group, both groups will
now have the same number of heads. For example: If you are told there
are two heads, the first group will have two coins, flip them both. If you
have taken both heads coins, and you flip them, there will now be no
heads in this group, there will also be none in the second group as you
have already taken both of those. If you have taken one heads and one

SOLUTIONS

tails, you flip both, this group will still have one heads. The remaining pile will also have one heads coin, as you removed only one of the two. Continue to try this with different numbers of coins and heads and you will see it always remains true.

DOE; CODE; DECOR; SCORED; RECORDS; CORRODES.

One quarter of the full length of the plank.

A single cut will fall either in the exact middle or in one half of the plank. We don't need to worry about which half, since you always end up with two parts of plank and we can always pick the smaller part to consider. Therefore, given we need to consider only half the plank, if you average many random cuts then on average they will appear in the middle of that one half that we always select; or in other words a quarter of the way along the total length of the original plank.

There are eleven: Chad, Cuba, Fiji, Iran, Iraq, Laos, Mali, Niue, Oman, Peru and Togo. (Though Sherlock would have only been able to name 8 as some of these went by different names at the time).

Cutlery.

He could not reach the top button; he was too short.

SOLUTIONS

You can try this out with two coins, and discover that there would be two rotations. This is because the upper gear is not only rolling around the other gear, but is also rolling around itself.

The letters were the last letters of each of the planets of the solar system in their order from the sun outwards: Mercury, Venus, Earth, Mars, Jupiter, Saturn, Uranus, and Neptune.

You simply stop imagining.

He should switch doors. At the start, he has a 1-in-3 chance of picking the correct door. Should he swap, he will have a 1-in-2 chance of picking the correct door. This is true only because the criminal will deliberately remove a door that he knows does not conceal the timer.

WATER: BREAKWATER and WATERPROOF; BOW: CROSSBOW and BOWLED; SUIT: SWIMSUIT and SUITCASE.

The fence.

SOLUTIONS

The lead. Any object submerged in water has an apparent weight loss equal to the weight of the fluid displaced. The gold is less dense than the lead and so takes up more volume than the lead for the same weight. Therefore, the gold will displace more water and thus will become lighter.

SNIPS/SPINS; STRESSED/DESSERTS; LOOTER/RETOOL.

Time.

It requires a mirror to be placed lengthways along the message. Once reflected, it reads "MEET ME HERE TONIGHT MY DEAR".

meet Me here tonight My dear

They were all musicians, playing for money throughout the night.

PERSIST, PRIESTS, STRIPES.

A deck of cards.

Thunder and lightning.

SOLUTIONS

Fire.

WAR; WARD; DRAWN; WANDER; WARDENS; ANSWERED.

They are noting the time of death using clock arithmetic, so, if read as 11:00 + 20 and 12:00 – 40, both agree that the time of death was 11:20.

TOOL: FOOTSTOOL and TOOLBAR; STRONG: HEADSTRONG and STRONGHOLD; HER: PANTHER and HERRINGS.

TRUST WATSON.

STRAINER, RESTRAIN, TERRAINS.

STEELS/SLEETS; REVILED/DELIVER; PEELS/SLEEP.

The first puppy had 15 spots; the second had 22 spots; the third had 27 spots.

A stamp.